CONTENTS

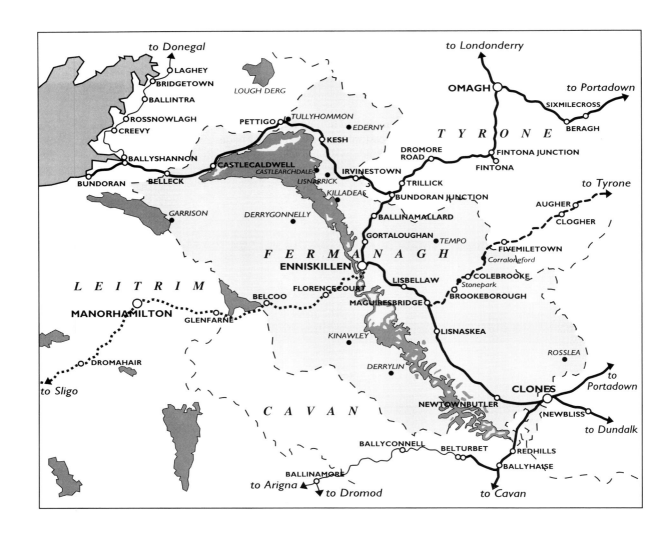

The Railways of County Fermanagh

———— Great Northern Railway (Ireland)
·············· Sligo, Leitrim and Northern Counties Railway
– – – – – Clogher Valley Railway
———— other railways

Fermanagh's Railways

A photographic tribute

Charles P Friel   Norman Johnston

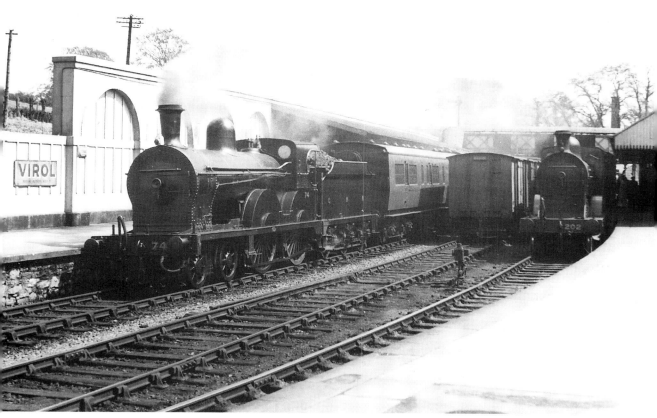

Enniskillen station in May 1956, viewed from the Omagh end of platform 1. On the right U class 4-4-0 No 202 *Louth* has just arrived in with the 10.45 am from Dundalk. Its coaches will become the 2.05 pm to Omagh. On the left a very clean PP class 4-4-0 No 74 has the Bundoran portion of this train, which will be added to it after No 202 goes on shed. No 74 was destined to be the last of this popular class to survive, facing the cutter's torch as late as 1964.

Charles Friel was born in Enniskillen and has been a life long railway enthusiast, active preservationist, photographer and collector of railway photographs. He is author of *Merlin* and *Slieve Gullion* and numerous railway articles. His illustrated talks on railways in the Ardhowen Theatre at Enniskillen have inspired this book. He is a Civil Servant by profession.

Norman Johnston has family roots in Fermanagh and is the grandson of a GNR Station Master. He has written several books including *The Fintona Horse Tram, The GNR in County Tyrone, The Norman Impact on the Medieval World* and *Peace, War and Neutrality 1935-49*. He is a retired school teacher and currently a publisher.

6 5 4 3 2 1

© Charles P Friel and Norman Johnston
Newtownards 1998

Designed by Colourpoint Books,
Newtownards
Maps drawn by Barry Craig
Printed by ColourBooks

ISBN 1 898392 39 0

Colourpoint Books
Unit D5, Ards Business Centre
Jubilee Road
NEWTOWNARDS
County Down
Northern Ireland
BT23 4YH
Tel: (01247) 820505/819787 Ex 239
Fax: (01247) 821900
E-mail: Info@colourpoint.co.uk
Web-site: www.colourpoint.co.uk

A note for the lay person

Readers of this book will see frequent references to 'Up' and 'Down' in relation to trains and platforms. In railway terminology the 'Up' direction is towards the line's headquarters. Thus on the GNR(I) 'Up' was towards Dublin (in Fermanagh, the Clones direction) and 'Down' towards Bundoran. On the SLNCR 'Up' was towards Enniskillen and 'Down' towards Sligo.
In signalling, a 'distant' signal was a yellow caution signal on the approaches to a station, a 'home' signal was a red stop signal controlling entry to it and a 'starter' signal was an identical red signal controlling departure from a station.

Front background photograph: The approaches to Enniskillen from Clones and Sligo.

Top: U class 4-4-0 No 204 *Antrim* at Enniskillen shed in 1956 in company with LQG 0-6-0 No 119 and PP 4-4-0 No 42.

Centre: U class 4-4-0 No 205 *Down* at Clones on the Up 'Bundoran Express' in August 1956.

Bottom: The 9 am Belfast-Enniskillen diesel arriving at Enniskillen in August 1956.

INTRODUCTION

Norman remembers

Fermanagh is rooted deep in my heart. I am linked to it by kinship, by memories and by the charm of its scenery and associations. The bones of my ancestors lie in its soil, and I frequently visit haunts that are as familiar to me today as they were over forty years ago when I was a child. I knew its railways well in my earliest years and travelled them frequently. Their closure in 1957 brought to me the first sense of bereavement I ever experienced. It was the loss of an old friend. Even today, as I travel the roads of Fermanagh, I can still see the trains — as vivid in my mind's eye as if it were only yesterday. Lisnagole accommodation crossing, on the lane down to my late uncle's farm of the same name, brings me back to days in the mid 1950s when, with my mother, I stood on the lane watching the Enniskillen-bound train passing, hauled by a clean and neat PP 4-4-0. Then, as the exhaust drifted away from the cutting 200 yards away, one of the Armstrong children, who lived in the gatehouse, ran out to open the gates for us. Or again, I stand on the derelict platform of Maguiresbridge station, where my grandfather William Johnston was briefly station master in 1918-20 before his untimely death, and look at the cottage, still occupied by Mr Traynor the last station master, where my father lived for those two years as a boy. I remember it as it used to be, and try to imagine it in 1920, with the Clogher Valley Railway connecting with the GNR trains and hustle and bustle going on in the transship shed, as goods were transferred between narrow gauge and standard gauge.

Railways, more than any other form of transport, seem to have a powerful effect on the emotions of many people. Fermanagh is no different in this respect. To this day, when the subject of the railways comes up in conversation, a room can grow uncannily quiet and eyes become a little misty. Then the sense of loss experienced all those years ago surfaces and someone says, "It's an awful shame they closed the railways. The train was a great way of getting about." Then they reminisce about going to school by train, about going to Bundoran on an excursion, and of seeing the 'Bundoran Express' with its clean, polished blue engine passing through Enniskillen at a breathtaking 5-10 mph, the proud name of Fermanagh's only named train hung on the smokebox — and it didn't even stop in Fermanagh! Other things can stimulate the memory. One is the sight and sound of a preserved steam engine — like 85 *Merlin* or 171 *Slieve Gullion* on the 'Portrush Flyer', both blue GNR locomotives — the rich aroma of soot and burnt oil, the hiss of the valves and

PP No 42 approaching Lisnagole accommodation crossing with the 4.30 pm mail train from Enniskillen. In the distance is the cutting, in which my mother, as a girl, was nearly killed by an unexpected train, while taking a short cut to school.

roar of the ejectors, the warmth of the firebox, the clank of the coupling rods — can all bring us back to childhood years in the 1940s or 1950s when these smells and sounds were everyday in Fermanagh.

Writing this book in cooperation with my co-author Charles Friel was a labour of love for us both. As teenagers we met in Portadown over thirty years ago and discovered not only a common love of trains, but a shared experience of Fermanagh and its railways. These two things led to a lifelong friendship, which has now resulted in this tribute to our favourite railways. As well as describing the history of the lines and illustrating them with our favourite pictures, we both felt an urge to put down on paper our own very personal feelings and memories of a great railway system. Not that these memories are particularly significant in themselves but we hope that, in sharing them, we will stir equally powerful memories within our readers.

I often meet railway enthusiasts who regret that they have no personal experience of Fermanagh's railways, and it makes me feel privileged and honoured that circumstances and ancestry put me in the position where I had. In some ways it is not surprising that Belfast people had little experience of railways in Fermanagh. An amazing number of people in Northern Ireland have never even been in Fermanagh. Fermanagh is not really on the way to anywhere if you live in the east of Ulster. You have to be going there to go to it, so to speak. Enniskillen is about two hours from Belfast by road. There is a somewhat fictitious story told about a conversation at a reception in Hillsborough Castle shortly after Sir Patrick Mayhew became N I Secretary. It goes something like this:

Mrs Mayhew:	And where are you from?
Fermanagh man:	I'm from Fermanagh
Mrs Mayhew:	Fermanagh. Mmm... Is that in the North or the South?
Fermanagh man:	No, it isn't. It's in the west.
Mrs Mayhew:	Well, I can't say I've heard of it. Is it near anywhere?
Fermanagh man:	No, it's not. We kinda keep ourselves to ourselves!

However, if you do go there, Fermanagh is a wonderful place. Known as 'Ulster's Lakeland', it is by far the most picturesque of the six Ulster counties that became part of Northern Ireland in 1921. It has close links with those other three Ulster counties – Monaghan, Cavan, and Donegal – which ended up in the Irish Free State at that time. With them it shared the self-reliance and independence of spirit that resulted from their remoteness from both Dublin and Belfast, and the cooperation that is characteristic of the 'border counties'. Fermanagh's railways crossed into all three of them as well as into its northern neighbour Tyrone, where I spent 25 happy years.

Fermanagh is dominated by its lakes and islands, which are a playground for both fishermen and weekend sailors. Upper and Lower Lough Erne, and the River Erne which links them, effectively divide the county in two. Those who live to the west of the county are often known as the folk 'beyond the lough' who have their own distinct dialect, different from but as unmistakably 'Fermanagh' as the accent in north-east Fermanagh. Wherever they live, Fermanagh folk are renowned for their friendliness and hospitality. It is virtually a cardinal sin to let someone, who calls at your house, leave without the obligatory 'cup of tea' (pronounced 'tay' in Fermanagh, in the French fashion). A 'cup of tea' means buns, scones, and buttered cake or fruit bread (brack) – in other words, the complete works – and refusal to accept is a matter of some offence!

Kinship is very important to Fermanagh folk. Relations are counted to second or third cousins, sometimes to once or twice removed as well. If you have any connection with the county, they will know your grandfather or your aunt or someone who 'belongs' to you. In the other five Northern Ireland counties Fermanagh folk living in exile have an especially warm spot for other Fermanagh folk. They seek each other out, have 'cups of tay' and talk knowledgeably about places like Derrygonnelly, Kinawley, Lisnarick and 'The Round O'. Since only about 60,000 people live in Fermanagh, everyone seems to know at least a quarter of the population. In this regard I am on firm ground. My father was a Johnston from Maguiresbridge and my mother a Moore from Lisnaskea. They spent the first half of their lives in Fermanagh, and came back there to live in their old age and eventually to be buried. Although they spent their married lives in Portadown, they brought me back to Fermanagh to be christened in the little country church in Maguiresbridge where they had been married eighteen months earlier. In 1994, within five months of each other, that same little church was the setting for their respective funeral services. To my mother, Fermanagh was always 'home', and although I have never actually lived there myself, I share that sense of belonging.

My first contact with the railways of Fermanagh was in April 1949 when my mother brought me from Portadown, via Clones, to Lisnaskea to be shown off to the relatives and to be christened in the 'right' county. Being only ten weeks old I didn't get the number of the engine! My father followed a few days later, travelling on the 5.35 pm to Derry as far as Omagh, from where he reached Lisnaskea via Enniskillen. This illustrated one superb feature of the Fermanagh lines — there were two alternative routes to Enniskillen, via Clones and via Omagh. This allowed a flexibility in travel arrangements and a wide choice of trains. Travelling from Portadown, you could go via Clones at 12 noon or 3.40 pm, and via Omagh at 5.45 pm.

I soon became a seasoned traveller. In 1949 alone I made the trip to Fermanagh six times, once by Omagh and the rest by Clones. This became the pattern in the years that followed, with additional local trips between Enniskillen and Lisnaskea. I never travelled on the Sligo Leitrim line, mainly because by parents had no relations in the Florencecourt-Belcoo area, but I did once venture onto the Bundoran branch. This was on 6 June 1953 when we took the 12 noon from Portadown to Omagh, changed to the Enniskillen train, changed again at Bundoran Junction and took the branch train as far as Irvinestown from which, after an hour's wait, we got a bus to our final destination, Lisnarick, where my mother's older sister lived. We retraced our steps a week later. A few years later this same aunt and her husband moved to a farm near Kesh, the front garden of which gave an excellent view of trains passing on the Bundoran branch. After the railway closed we used to walk the line at this point and in 1961 I remember a UTA UG class 0-6-0 on the lifting train.

As soon as I could talk, my father set about broadening my education. Coming from a railway family, he was a mine of information about trains. I learnt all about signals and the procedures for starting a train. The Fermanagh journeys were used to teach me about steam engines. I would be stood on the platform next the engine and taught the names of all the bits from the chimney down to the coupling rods. I think the first six words I learnt were 'Daddy, Mummy, dome, whistle, home and distant', in roughly that order, the last two referring to signals rather than the house and relatives!

It was in Fermanagh too that I was presented with my first train set. Having messed about with various unsatisfactory O gauge clockwork trains, I had discovered Hornby-Dublo electric trains, being often found glued to the display cabinet in Jeffers shop in Portadown. So a letter was duly sent to Santa coming up to Christmas 1956, and on Christmas morning in Lisnagole farmhouse there it was — A4 4-6-2 *Silver King* and two gleaming red and cream coaches, with an oval of track and, as an extra bonus from my financially hard-pressed father, a siding and three wagons as well! How he ever got this lot smuggled down to Fermanagh on the train without me noticing, still exercises my mind. Mind you, Lisnagole had no electricity, so trying it out had to wait until we got back to Gilford, the village near Portadown where we lived, up to 1957.

Many images of rail travel to Fermanagh are still very vivid in my mind. I especially remember Clones, which was a very large station by the standards of the GNR. It was a busy junction where the routes from Dundalk and Portadown converged before continuing over the border into Fermanagh. In addition, there was a branch to Cavan on the Down side. Passengers from Portadown had to change into the train from Dundalk to Enniskillen, if they wanted to go to Fermanagh. With customs clearance, this usually involved waiting half an hour or more for the connection. Often the Up train from Enniskillen would arrive during this delay, also making connection with the Portadown train and the branch train from Cavan. Clones had a third road between the Up and Down platforms, and the station pilot often sat in here, ready to make a quick shunt of a parcels van from one train to another.

I remember on one such occasion sitting with my parents in the Enniskillen train at Platform 1 waiting for customs clearance. GNR third class carriages were centre corridor with two bays of eight seats to each compartment, every other bay having a door. Each window, whether with door or not, consisted of two side lights and a drop light window. I had the drop light open in our compartment and was leaning out watching all the bustle at Platforms 2/3 (the island platform). I remember the station pilot arriving right beside us on the middle road with the cab just at our window. It was a big black engine — possibly an LQG or SG3 0-6-0 or perhaps a Q class 4-4-0 — and the driver, having a spare moment, put chat on us. I remember him saying, "Would you like to see the fire, son?" and with that he threw open the firebox door, only six feet away. It was most impressive with the blast of heat that hit my face and this huge blazing furnace, much bigger even than my uncle's Wellstood cooker. Then his fireman threw a shovel of coal into the back and he slammed the door shut.

After the wait in Clones, the train then left, but, at Newtownbutler, faced another delay with the British

A busy scene at the Dundalk end of Clones on 16 June 1951 at 6.30 pm. In the foreground is No 107, in the middle road between platforms 1 and 2. Trains are waiting to depart to Dundalk (top) and Portadown (middle), the latter hauled by QL 4-4-0 No 156.

customs. My father as always good at finding the best train to use, and one of his favourites was the new direct Portadown-Enniskillen (via Clones) diesel train introduced in 1953. It can be seen on the front cover arriving at Enniskillen. The GNR had helped pioneer diesel traction in the British Isles and, in 1950, introduced a fleet of ten three-coach AEC diesel trains. These were widely used on a variety of services. The new train left Portadown at 12.10 pm, travelling by Clones, and reaching Enniskillen at about 2 pm, returning at 3 pm. This avoided having to change trains at Clones. On 29 December 1953, I remember travelling on the return working from Enniskillen as far as Lisnaskea. We were travelling with my father's brother Joseph and his wife and son. The first class compartments in these trains faced front and allowed a panoramic view of the line ahead. The train was far from crowded and, by some arrangement or other, the guard let us travel first class (Joseph worked for British Railways and my father for the UTA, which may have counted for something). Anyway my cousin Colin and I took up position in the very front, directly behind the GNR driver. To improve the view even more, we *stood* on the first class seats. To this day I can remember the look of disapproval which the driver bestowed upon us when he noticed what we were doing. As we shrank down in our seats Colin said innocently "I wonder what's bothering him?" But we had a fair idea and behaved ourselves the rest of the way! The following day we caught the same diesel at 3.25 pm in Lisnaskea and were in Portadown by 5.30 pm, a saving of nearly an hour on the usual train. In the summer this train ran much earlier, at 9.00 am, and started at Belfast, reaching Clones at 10.57 am and Enniskillen at 11.37 am, certainly much faster than by road. The return working was at 12.30 pm.

In case the reader is remarking on what a head for detail I had at the age of four, I will let you into a secret — my father kept a diary! I now own all these diaries and with hindsight it is remarkably fortunate that my father recorded his travel arrangements so meticulously. He usually noted what trains he travelled on, though never, unfortunately, the engine number.

One very frequently used diesel in our family was the 6.20 pm from Enniskillen to Clones. This was a useful service for anyone who had spent the afternoon in Enniskillen and found catching the 5.00 pm steam train a trifle tight. This train was either a railbus or a Gardner articulated railcar like No C3. This vehicle dated from 1935, and was a regular on the Bundoran branch in the winter. The railbus features in the photographic section and was a genuine road bus, with steel flanged wheels at the front and a steel tyre placed over its pneumatic tyre at the back. I have come across many dated photographs of the 6.20 pm and often check my father's diary to see if by chance I might have been on it. The closest I have come is a Colin Hogg photograph taken on 22 August 1955, exactly a week after I had travelled on it!

Of all the stations that are etched in my mind's eye, I suppose Lisnaskea is the one that has the most poignant memories. Perhaps this is because so many journeys started and ended there. It was one of the smallest of the Irish North stations and apparently the least photographed. Lisnaskea consisted of a single platform on the Up side, with a passing loop and a level crossing at the Down end just past the points. Like many other GNR stations in Fermanagh, the name 'LISNASKEA' was cast in large whitewashed concrete letters set into the bank opposite the platform. The only other trackwork was a single siding (with headshunt) into the goods shed on the Up side, trailing from the Newtownbutler end. This meant that wagons for Lisnaskea could most easily be shunted by the Up goods but I never saw this, as it came through at 6.15 am in the morning.

I only once ever saw the loop being used, mainly because we usually travelled on the early afternoon or evening trains. However I can pinpoint the date from my father's diary — it was on Monday 5 November 1956, when we rather unusually took the 10.09 am to Clones (8.25 am ex-Omagh). I remember watching the Down goods being shunted into the loop on this occasion. However this was a daily occurrence, as the 8.55 am goods from Clones always crossed the 8.25 am Omagh to Dundalk passenger at Lisnaskea, where the goods stopped over for 40 minutes. By leaving the goods in the loop the engine could run round and add wagons from Lisnaskea to the rear of the train, should that be needed.

The very last occasion I ever used Lisnaskea station, or indeed travelled on any Fermanagh train, was on Saturday 24 August 1957, just seven weeks before the line closed. It was a dreadful day, with heavy rain, and a fierce storm, and we were returning on the 5 pm from Enniskillen, which got into Lisnaskea at 5.26 pm, having started at Derry at 1.35 pm and would reach Dundalk at 7.45 pm. We walked the half mile from my aunt's house to the station with our luggage and took refuge in the waiting room, the window of which gave a view of the level crossing and the approaching train. In normal weather we would have waited on the platform. I remember consciously thinking "I want to remember this moment. This is the last time I will ever travel on this line." So I drank in the experience, and I can still see the train coming in over the level crossing and slowing for the platform, as we stood watching from the window. The engine was small and black with a tall chimney, so I know with hindsight that it was a PP 4-4-0.

I was in Portadown on the night of the actual closure of the Fermanagh lines — 30 September 1957. The line from Portadown to Clones was closing the same night and, as the last train came in from Clones, detonators placed on the line near Portadown shed exploded in the usual railwaymen's tribute to last trains. We heard them up in the house and our first reaction was that it was an IRA raid on the police station (An IRA campaign had begun earlier in the year, particularly affecting Fermanagh). However a few seconds later my father realised a more likely explanation for the explosions, "Of course, it's the last train on the Armagh line", he said.

At the time the shock of the closures took a long time to sink in at family level. For a long period there was an optimistic hope that wiser councils would prevail, and the lines would be reopened in due course. Throughout 1958-9 my mother resolutely kept saying, "As long as the tracks are not lifted there's hope." For those two years they lay derelict and weeds began to grow among the rails. On 1 October 1958 the old GNR was split up between the UTA and CIE, but this made little impact in Fermanagh, though in Portadown, from the middle of 1959, the GNR mahogany-coloured coaches began to appear in UTA green. Thankfully, only six of the blue engines were repainted black in 1961-2 and a few survived to 1965 in GNR sky blue.

Now and then, if we happened to be in Enniskillen on market day, we would look in at Enniskillen station

Lisnaskea station in 1962. The goods shed in the background later became part of Mealiff's garage.

and take a walk down its forlorn platforms. At Lisnaskea, my cousin Sandra and I sometimes walked the half mile down to the station and explored its ghostly atmosphere. The UTA had begun using it as a stabling point for its buses. Travelling to Fermanagh, particularly Lisnaskea, now became problematical for the family. Ever faithful to rail travel, we took the train to Omagh, from where, after a wait, there was a bus to Enniskillen. The buses were often the traditional Leyland PS1 or PS2 34 seat single deckers, but in those days the Omagh-Enniskillen road was poor and I really did not look forward to these trips. I was always sick on the bus and positively miserable. The 25 miles to Enniskillen were continuous Z-bends and I felt every one! At Enniskillen the journey was still not over as we had to get a local UTA bus via Maguiresbridge or an Erne bus on the direct Enniskillen-Lisnaskea road. As we huddled at Enniskillen bus depot on winter days (it was nowhere as hospitable as its modern counterpart) we thought longingly of the direct Portadown to Enniskillen GNR diesel, and silently cursed the Northern Ireland government for its short-sighted transport policy.

Little wonder that we often opted for the lazy option of taking a lift in one of my Uncle Robert Donaldson's Erne Engineering Company's Ford cars which, in the days before car-carriers, were actually driven new from the docks in Belfast by young apprentices of the Erne. This procedure involved a car with four drivers going to Belfast and returning in three brand new cars. Uncle Robert could arrange for a driver to detour to our house in Portadown (no motorway in those days!), pick us up and drop us in Lisnaskea. Of course this only worked if there happened to be cars going on the day we needed to travel. Thus it was that in the 1958-62 era we got to sample quite a wide variety of Henry Ford's Dagenham products! It was an interesting sort of lottery, as you never knew quite what to expect. It could be a black side-valve Ford Popular, with the prewar body shell, a Prefect, one of the new 1959 Anglias or, if we were lucky, a Consul or Zephyr. On one occasion in 1958, I well remember the driver arriving in an absolutely brand new light green upright Anglia, a model phased out in 1953. It even had shiny clear plastic taped over the seats. The story was that it was for an elderly lady in Enniskillen who had one before and who found the new model much too new-fangled. Ford had actually gone to the trouble of building a one-off Anglia to please her!

However, I digress from the subject, though I am making the point that the closure of Fermanagh's railways led to a much poorer availability of transport. Journeys took longer and were much less comfortable.

Easter 1960 was, as usual, spent in Lisnaskea. By this time the line had been closed over two and a half years. I was playing in the garden with my cousin one afternoon when we heard the distinct whistle of a steam engine. But it was no ghost train. Down at the level crossing gates, which were within sight of the house, was a steam locomotive! We dashed into the house shouting, "There's a train down at the station!" And of course everyone came out to see. It was in fact the lifting train, which at that time was lifting the Clones to Lisnaskea section. The very last occasion that I ever saw a train in Fermanagh was the following Easter, which was spent at Kesh, in my other aunt's house at Dromard, beside the Bundoran Branch. On 6-7 April 1961 the lifting train passed three times. On the Thursday I presumably saw it returning to Omagh in the evening, and on the Friday it passed in the morning heading towards Kesh and again in the evening returning. I remember getting a friendly wave from the fireman. That was the very end of the railway as far as I was concerned. The next time I was back the tracks had all gone. In 1962 my Kesh aunt was obliged by the government to buy (at minimal cost) the portion of the Bundoran branch that passed through her land. Apparently the owner of the farm in 1866 had sold the same land to the Enniskillen, Bundoran and Sligo Railway a century earlier. Many farmers were given the same deal in the early 1960s. On a holiday recently I met a retired Civil Servant who had been involved in administering these sales, and she confirmed what I always suspected — that the purpose of these sales was to make sure that the lines could never possibly be reopened.

As a final personal postscript, I often regret that I did not persuade my father to take even one photograph of the railways in his native county. In those days money was tight and he rationed himself to one eight-exposure film a year. I began my own photography in 1962 when it was too late, though my first ever photograph was appropriately at Omagh station, while waiting for a bus to Enniskillen. One day in 1967, when I was into colour slide photography, my Lisnaskea cousin and I, now adults, walked down to the

Lisnaskea station in 1967. It was demolished the following year.

remains of the old station, derelict but still standing. We wandered along the overgrown platform and through the ticket office and entrance hall. Then we entered the old waiting room and there in front of me was the window through which in August 1957 I had watched the 5 pm from Enniskillen arriving to take me on my last trip on Fermanagh's railways. It was a very sad moment as I looked through the by now glassless window at the empty trackbed and the road where the gates had been. But I could still see the train and it brought a lump to my throat. Today the edge of Carrowshee housing estate occupies the site of the old station and the children who play there probably don't even know that trains once passed by. The only bit still standing is the goods shed, now part of Mealiff's garage. After leaving the station, my cousin and I walked towards the town and then turned right to reach the bridge that carried a minor road over the railway. The slide I took is reproduced above. It shows the station buildings and the trackbed and by a happy irony may well be the only colour picture ever taken of Lisnaskea station. If any reader has a photograph of Lisnaskea station in black and white or colour, I would dearly love them to get in touch with me.

Charles Remembers

I sometimes wonder if I was born listening to a steam engine at work!

Away back in the late summer of 1946, I was born in the County Hospital in Enniskillen. 'The County', as we always seemed to call it, was on a hill between the Tempo Road and the railway. There is a Sandown Home there nowadays. The maternity ward was on the first floor, in the corner overlooking the Sligo Leitrim and Northern Counties Railway's yard. The joint SLNCR and Great Northern passenger station was beyond that and the GNR engine shed off to the right. Indeed, the first photograph taken of me was on the balcony of that ward with my godparents. I was just three days old and about to be whisked off to be christened — they didn't hang about in those days! No matter how I try to print the negative, I can't get any of the railway into it!

My parents lived at Wickham Drive, a terrace of eight three-storey houses which is now the Belmore Court Motel. We lived at No 2, which later became No 7 Tempo Road, when the imposition of postcodes rationalised all sorts of addresses and almost wiped out our townland names. The Tempo Road was at the back of the house and the Dublin Road (renamed the Belfast Road since then) ran at the bottom of the long gardens at the front of the houses. The house was, in a way, almost surrounded by railways. From the front of the house you could see the Sligo Leitrim and, from the top room at the back of the house, you could see part of the passenger station.

When I was about three, I had the impression that there was another station in Enniskillen! My mother's youngest brother emigrated to America. He left from our house and I got the idea that he had gone all the way by train. Soon after that I was ill and spent a day or two in my parents' bedroom at the front of the house. From there I could see steam sometimes billowing about the Taylor Woods nylon factory. I put two and two together and came to the conclusion that this modern-looking building was the station for America!

But back to reality and what we *really* saw from the front of the house. Trains from Sligo came across the Weirs Bridge and the Dublin Road before coming into view. They skirted the edge of the Castlecoole Woods on what appeared to be a high embankment above the houses of Lower Celtic Park, before disappearing from view behind the Model School. I have few memories of seeing railbuses or the railcar on this high bit of track but even a six year old could not help noticing the many long trains of cattle wagons, each complete with a brake van, which, to our untutored eyes, was known as 'a last wagon'. The incoming cattle or goods trains sometimes stopped alongside the Woods and we would watch for a small lineside fire once they had moved off.

The view from the top room at the back of the house was, if anything, even more interesting. You had to look past Forde's garage (later West's) and across the top of the one-storey chicken hatchery, now a three-storey hotel. There was a distant, almost side-on, view of the yellow footbridge, some of the main passenger buildings on its left and part of the engine shed area to the right.

I am the eldest of three children and, in the days before I started school, my mother (probably to get peace to attend to Mary and John) would send me up to the top room "to watch the puff puffs". I needed a tin box to stand on but the ploy worked every time. One very early memory is of watching an engine blowing off vigorously and being fascinated to see what would happen to the tall column of steam when it met the footbridge.

My first railway journey was just after Christmas 1946 when my parents brought me to my mother's family home near Mullaghmore in north Sligo. This was my introduction to train travel and where better than on the Bundoran branch? We came back to Enniskillen in early January, just before the big snow of 1947 closed everything down.

From my mother's diaries, I see that we were on the train to Bundoran again on 30 July, coming home on 19 August. Then, just a couple of days before my first birthday, we travelled with my father's mother, brother and sister to their house in Rossnakill in north Donegal. Our route was, of course, via Omagh and on

The east side of Enniskillen from the Cole Monument about 1920. In the foreground is the Fair Green, with part of Gaol Square on the extreme right. The 'v' of the junction between the Tempo Road (left) and Dublin Road (right) contains the Masonic Hall. Wickham Drive is further down the Tempo Road on the same side. The terrace of houses to the left is Westville. Away to the right is Lower Celtic Park, with the Castlecoole Woods beyond.

to Strabane, where we changed into a narrow gauge train for Letterkenny. The journey was completed in a Lough Swilly bus on the Fanad route. We retraced our steps just under three weeks later. Not surprisingly, I have no recollection of these pioneering trips, though my brother and I later distinguished Donegal railcars from Great Northern ones by our ability to see out the front of the former. I remember thinking, in later years, that the Donegal cars were safer, since they had the entrance door at the top of the steps rather than at the bottom (as in Railcar C^1). The doorwell in C^1 struck me as a dangerous place to drop a toy.

My strongest railway memories from before I started school centre on the frequent afternoon walks out the Tempo Road with Mary, John and my mother. En route we passed the Breandrum Cemetery on one side and 'the County' with its tennis courts, on the other. My mother would sometimes recall playing tennis here in her nursing days and the long searches for lost balls amongst the graves. Slightly further on, the Sligo Leitrim's engine sheds came into view, where the railway was on an embankment about twelve feet high. Lockingtons had a coal yard here and received coal from wagons at the top of the embankment. These wagons were unloaded by simply shovelling the coal over the side where it cascaded down the embankment; indeed the whole embankment seemed to be made of coal. I remember being fascinated at how each shovelful of coal kept its shape as it arched through the air, before it landed with a light, flittering sound and scattered about the middle of the hill.

Then our walk brought us under the Sligo Leitrim's metal bridge where little seemed to happen. Beyond this bridge, though, the Tempo Road ran parallel to the GNR's Clones line for about half a mile, before the road dog-legged over the railway on another bridge at the outer end of the Killynure siding. This was a metal bridge, built to accommodate double track and the siding made use of this by finishing a few yards on the Clones side of the bridge with a square buffer, built of sleepers and earth, I think. The bridge, with its handrails and high-domed rivets, was painted a blue-grey colour which had fascinating silvery sparkling specks embedded in its mirror-smooth finish. I was told once that this was a painting system that involved electrically-charged metallic paint being sprayed onto metal with an opposite charge. This was well beyond me at the time — and still is, a bit! Some of the bigger boys from Wickham Drive used this bridge to try and either spit into or drop stones down the engines' chimneys. I was always too young for this hooliganism (thank goodness) and knew only the simpler delight of hoping to see a train.

One glorious memory is of seeing Driver Jimmy Kelly storming alongside the Tempo Road as he left with a passenger train for Clones. He was on our side of the cab and waving what looked like a white hankie to us as he passed. I can remember that there was much whistling and the engine had a tall chimney, so it might have been a P or a PP class locomotive. Mr Kelly lived in Lower Celtic Park with his wife Kate and daughter Angela. Mrs Kelly came from near Tullaghan in north Leitrim and had, by a remarkable coincidence, been at National School with my mother.

The Killynure siding diverged from the Clones line just past the access road to another tennis court. The siding often had about ten or twenty goods wagons. Some were wagons of coal for Lockingtons. The others were probably waiting for attention at the town's relatively small goods yard. The siding was about three quarters of a mile from our house and probably at a point where four-year-old legs were likely to be giving up. I do not know whether or not this was the reason for my 'job' here; I had to call out the wagon numbers and read any words or letters on the wagons. One afternoon there was big excitement — there was an engine in the siding! I remember us watching it make several attempts to lift a rake of wagons in the siding. Each time the engine started away there were angry shouts and cross words as the men realised that they didn't have all of the rake with them. There was much crashing of buffers and ringing of couplings before all were safely gathered in. My mother explained that 'the bad boys' had undone the couplings!

There was an interesting sequel to this story over 45 years later. I was giving an illustrated talk in Enniskillen's splendid Ardhowen Theatre, to commemorate the 40th anniversary of the closure of the railways. I recounted the above incident and thought little of it. Afterwards, though, one of the audience, a man of about my own years and who had then lived in Westville, told me how young fellas from around there used to play in the Sligo Leitrim yard on a Sunday when no-one was about. One of the things they used to do was undo as many wagon couplings as they could. This man went on to tell me that his mother had once given him a terrible telling off for being with 'the bad boys' who did this. And, 45 years later, when I recounted my story, he could hear his mother telling him how disappointed she was with him. And there he was, sitting in the audience at the Ardhowen, going red in the face and the sweat breaking on him as he felt guilty all over again!

Family Sunday afternoon walks were often out the Castlecoole Road which crossed over the SLNCR line. But the Sligo trains hardly ever ran on Sundays and, anyway, the attention of the young Friels was directed towards a flock of red and black hens in a small yard that backed onto the line. Our walk then lay through the grounds of Castlecoole, a large 18th century mansion and the home of Lord Belmore. Here the concrete bases of army huts were still visible and there was a concrete roadway, a legacy of wartime military use. I remember a Red Cross fête in the grounds of Castlecoole, probably about 1953. One stallholder had a baseboard with an oval of Hornby 0 gauge track and a black clockwork tank engine. Around the outer edge of the track, short lengths had labels for many of the stations between Enniskillen

The author with his sister Mary on the Tempo Road one Sunday afternoon. In the top left corner is the accommodation crossing which gave access to the tennis court and marked the start of the Killynure siding.

U class 4-4-0 No 202 *Louth* passes the Killynure siding with a train from Clones. The ground frame controlling access to the siding is in the foreground. To the right the Tempo Road follows the line, before crossing it at the far end of the siding.

and Bundoran and there were also blank spaces between each label. The idea was that you put a penny at the 'station' where you thought the engine would stop and, if you were right, you won another penny! It is now all too obvious that partial winding by the operator could have resulted in very few wins, but those were simpler times.

But back to those Sunday walks. Before reaching Castlecoole House itself, we took a different road out of the estate and this brought us onto the Dublin Road near the Weirs Bridge. The line crossed the Dublin Road on a metal bridge with a stone pier in the middle of the road. There was something of a bad bend on the approach from the Enniskillen direction and we were always cautioned about crossing the road hereabouts. Sometime about 1955, a motorcyclist was killed when he failed to take the corner properly and hit the stone pier.

It was said that the Weirs Bridge was unsafe and a cautionary tale was often told of a woman who took a short cut across the bridge and fell through rotten boards. This tale was more relevant to older children who were known to be tempted to walk the track on a trainless Sunday afternoon. Sadly, I have no memories of seeing anything cross the bridge though I did cross it a few times, of which more later. The area below the bridge was a magnet for people out for a Sunday stroll. We usually played or just sat around under the trees while others swam and dived in the river. You had to be a big boy to do that and there was something approaching a scandal when one swimmer cut his foot on broken glass and got a terrible infection.

The other big scandal from those days was when the new fire station at the junction of the Tempo and Dublin Roads was being built around 1953. The building has a steel frame and men building that frame worked on Sundays! This shock news was greeted with a knowing shake of the head and "What else could you expect?" when it became known that they were from Belfast! After the fire station opened, all the young Wickham Drivers became very interested in fire engines and, any time the siren went, we would all race down to the end of the Tempo Road to watch the fun as the firemen appeared from around the town. In those days they either came running, or on bicycles which were abandoned and sent crashing into each other or the wall next Westville. I remember being intrigued at how long the engines were away at the big fire at Florencecourt, home of the Earls of Enniskillen, in March 1955. At one time, fire engines were almost as big a draw as the railway!

From about 1950 onwards, we used the trains quite a lot. Our travel pattern was to go to my mother's home place in the first few days of July and come back in early August. Those Sligo holidays were idyllic. We had the run of the farm and helped with all sorts of jobs. We had the sea and a superb beach almost to ourselves (although it was always called a 'strand' then). We came home complete with Sligo accents and a compulsion to say "hello" to everyone we met. This was fair enough in Enniskillen but played not nearly so well once we had moved to Portadown. Those summers also included about ten days in Donegal. These became less frequent after 1953 but the trips to Sligo increased. From 1952 (when we all had had chicken pox and my mother thought we could do with building up) we spent our Easter holidays in Sligo as well. From about then too, I was big enough to go on the one-day visits to Sligo before Christmas to deliver presents. The first of these gave me quite a shock. Compared to the balmy days of summer hay-making, climbing trees and playing in the sand, everywhere was very bare, very cold and very wet!

All of these journeys involved using the train. Getting on to the station platform in Enniskillen seemed something akin to storming a castle, to my young eyes. Guarding the way to the trains was a big door that was slammed shut before departure and then a bell was rung before the guard blew his whistle and the train moved off. One summer, maybe 1954, I was sent up to the station to meet my father's mother who was coming from England. She didn't arrive via Clones but she did arrive shortly afterwards off the Omagh train. And rather than idle about the platform to wait between trains, I sat on the steps outside, in the sun. I sometimes wonder what I missed!

Easter trips to Bundoran always seemed to involve a change at the Junction into Railcar C[1]. This was relatively easy to do as it did not involve getting bulky suitcases across the footbridge but it was a different matter on the way home.

Railcar C[1] on the branch presented something of a tactical problem in that it did not have any 'facilities'. I remember my brother and I getting very excited when we thought that the distaff side of the party was about to be left behind in the ladies room at the Junction. The railcar was noisy and smelly, I am told. We were oblivious to that but I do remember it being cold. One Good Friday (and it might be as far back as our first Easter trip in 1952), we got as far as Belleek when we set back away from the platform into the short loop and waited for something coming the other way. I cannot recall what that was. It might have been the seemingly never photographed Pettigo permanent way lorry, as a cattle special seems unlikely on that day. Anyway, I clearly remember the long wait and looking across at the Leitrim mountains and seeing them covered in snow. Easter was quite early that year. My mother's comment was "What are we letting ourselves in for?".

Good Friday afternoon in Bundoran was something else in the mid-fifties. The long wait for the connecting Great Northern Derry to Sligo bus, for the final seven miles or so, was like an extra penance. The place was like a graveyard, there was nothing open and the Atlantic wind had something extra in its cutting edge. The shops had yet to get their fresh coat of paint for the summer trade and a swinging rusty metal sign screeching near the Hollyrood Hotel summed the whole thing up — echoing, deserted, and desolate.

It can now be told, though, that not everything in Bundoran was bolted and shut on that fiercely cold Good Friday. The side door to one bar was open and I remember my mother getting a warming sherry while we got orange minerals. In those days soft drinks were served in very tall and slowly tapering glasses that had huge heavy blobs of glass for bases. And as you drank you left a scattering of orange bits down the glass, unless you swilled them off (a dangerous thing to do) or tried to suck them up with your straw (strangely unsatisfactory). They don't seem to have orange bits these days.

We became quite familiar with the railway, sometimes to the point of embarrassing my mother. Maybe I should mention that we usually travelled without my father. His job meant that he sometimes came at Easter and, in the summer, he would join us for the last two weeks before we came home. Once my mother mentioned anything about an approaching customs post, we would set up a chorus about the customs men coming and generally get excited. It wasn't that my mother was ever 'carrying' much (to use the vernacular) that would be of interest to these bogey men. But she got embarrassed when others looked at her askance and seemed to anticipate some fun when the arch interrogators came through the train.

"If you stood on the seats after leaving the station . . ." A PP 4-4-0 is seen leaving Ballyshannon for Bundoran. On the right background, amidst the clouds, are the profiles of Benviskin (left) and Truskbeg (right), with the Leitrim mountains above the train itself.

The customs post at Ballyshannon, on the way to Bundoran, was something different, though. If you stood on the seats after leaving the station you eventually got a glimpse of the yellow tops of the huge sandy banks of Tullan strand behind Finner army camp — proof, at last, that we were getting near the sea. The journey was nearly over and the holiday could really begin! I remember being very disappointed in 1957, on our final journey to Bundoran, when we couldn't stand on the seats. There were too many others in the train and, anyway, wasn't I getting a bit big for this?

Other memories of the branch are of those delightful wooden centre corridor carriages with the bevelled circular windows in the intermediate doors that could swing both ways and the knurled door knobs that were just fascinating! Once, though, I can remember looking through broken bits of floor at the grey ballast flying past below. There were landmarks to look out for, too, such as the petrol luggage trolley — 'the bogie' — that echoed its way around the platforms at Bundoran Junction, the glimpse of Lough Erne just before Castlecaldwell or the Fiddler's Stone soon afterwards. The set-back signal cabin at Belleek, with the pottery's disappearing siding, was always intriguing. Belleek also had that tunnel under the main street and the crossing of the Erne.

Bundoran always held the promise that the train would actually run in under the roof rather that stand far out near the engine release crossover. As the biggest child, I had the job of helping lug the huge suitcases off the train, so where we stopped really made a difference! Inside the station, right behind the buffers, was a small Easons bookstall selling papers, magazines, sweets, and cigarettes. We were sometimes told the story of an engine hitting the buffers so hard that the bookstall fell over, but I've never been able to get any confirmation of this, even from Mrs Kelly who had worked there before moving to Enniskillen.

As I have said, journeys to and from Sligo involved the Great Northern's Derry to Sligo bus. There was always a chance that the bus conductor would be Jimmy McGloin, a neighbour of my mother's family. It was something of a bone of contention, though, that the Derry to Sligo bus left Bundoran at 4.25 pm while the 3.00 pm from the Junction didn't arrive until 4.36 pm! Unless the Derry bus was running late, this meant a wait until 6.30 pm. The connection was mercifully better in the opposite direction when all hands were inevitably feeling quite upset. Waiting for a bus at Bundoran often meant hiding from the wind in the glass shelter to the left of the entrance doorway and the bus would simply pick us up by doing a circle in front of the station. Thankfully we seldom had to use the highly inadequate bus park on the hill overlooking the station. There the shelters were simply V-shaped roofs set about nine feet in the air and nothing else! Whoever designed the place had obviously never been near it on an average day in summer, let alone in the winter. The buses in this park could be something of a variety, for there were visiting UTA green and white buses, alongside GNR buses going to strange places like Carrick on Shannon or Portnoo. I had no idea where either place was but the latter sounded exotic, a place full of pirates and buried treasure. If you know Portnoo, I'll leave you to draw your own conclusions as to how accurate my impressions were!

Very occasionally we got to Bundoran by using the Erne Bus Service, better known as Cassidy's buses. Cassidy had a route along the southern shore of Lower Lough Erne. I remember once the driver was Johnny Goan and the conductor was Peter Cadden, who later lived in Portadown for a time. The road was very bumpy indeed in those days and there was an emergency stop at one point to allow one of the young Friels to be sick.

Two other Great Northern bus journeys could be mentioned here. Firstly, during our holidays we went by GNR bus to church in Cliffoney each Sunday morning. This was a Ballyshannon to Sligo working that had the added attraction of usually being a double-decker in both directions! For other journeys to Sligo, to see cousins or to go shopping, we were back to the single deckers. Secondly, there were day trips from Enniskillen to Derrynacreeve, south of Swanlinbar, on the GNR's route to Cavan. My father's mother had come from there originally and my father sometimes went to visit relations on a Saturday, bringing some of us with him. The outward run started at Enniskillen station and went through the town, but I felt lost once we reached the Sligo Road! The return working was a Saturdays-only service which got us back to Enniskillen railway station at 7.25 pm. I remember some of those journeys after dark, with the afterglow of sunset backlighting the Cuilcagh mountains and giving the scene a haunted and spooky feeling. All of these

A line up of GNR buses at Ballyshannon garage on 14 August 1948. From left to right we have No 274 (a 1930 Leyland Lion, originally 119); No 302, a 1934 Leyland, with GNR body, but rebuilt with a Gardner engine; No 218, a similar GNR-built 1937 Gardner; and Nos 434 and 437, both AEC Regent II double deckers, built in 1948 with Park Royal bodies.

journeys have combined to make the sound of a Gardner diesel engine quite nostalgic. Even though I seldom found the silvery wire-covered and hooded Clayton heater provided much in the way of heat, GNR buses had a very solid wooden feel and sound that was sadly absent elsewhere. And I have not since heard the distinctive dull and vibrating buzzing and ringing mixture of sounds produced by the bell in the driver's cab of a GNR bus. The dull creamy yellow and orange glow of the deco-designed light shades only added to their magic.

Another journey from Enniskillen, but by rail this time, was the shopping trip to Blacklion, probably made before I started school. Several wives from Wickham Drive would occasionally head off on the 1.45 pm railbus for Sligo and get off at Belcoo. My highlights of the journey were to look out for our house as we passed through the Castlecoole Woods and then the thrill of crossing the Weirs Bridge and looking down into the dark waters or across to the trees where we had played. The Weirs Bridge was much higher than its Belleek counterpart, which seemed so much tamer. Once arrived in Belcoo, we walked across the border to Blacklion and, after visiting a couple of shops, I would find my coat pockets bulging with tea or sugar. I don't know what else was bought. I didn't ask and wasn't told.

These trips were made during the winter and the return from Blacklion to Belcoo was made under the cover of darkness and in total silence. The dreaded customs post was a grey caravan, like the ones used by County Council roadmen and it was parked at the side of the road. I remember that we had to walk in the middle of the road so as not to scrunch the small stones at the side. Once we had successfully tip-toed past this, the rest of the walk to Belcoo station was plain sailing and we made our way to the far platform to wait for the railcar from Sligo. The waiting room was lit by a single oil lamp and I remember one local youth taking great delight in repeatedly running in and blowing it out! After that endurance test, the almost-new Railcar B on the 4.00 pm out of Sligo — and another close encounter with a Gardner engine — was most welcome.

In the summer of 1955 there was a break with tradition and I went to Sligo by car. The car was an A35 belonging to a friend of my mother's. I sat on my father's knee in the front passenger seat; how times have changed! I had the job of working the indicator knob which was mounted in the centre of the dashboard near the windscreen. I can't imagine that my services were needed much. The biggest memory of that trip was the approach to Ballyshannon close to what I now know were Camlin gates, where the Bundoran branch was on an embankment and quite close to the road. About a hundred yards on the Belleek side of the gates, we met a train coming out from Bundoran. Again the tall chimney made a strong impression, as did the string of mahogany coaches.

My father's job took us away from Enniskillen in October 1955 when he was transferred to Portadown. The plan had been to travel by train via Clones and Armagh. Unfortunately, on the day, the furniture movers arrived late (another black mark for Belfast men!) and we missed the train. We ended up travelling to Portadown squashed into the cab of the furniture lorry. Thus disappeared my last chance to travel over that part of the Irish North and we never did.

Living in Portadown was very different from Enniskillen. We needed to get a tinny UTA bus to and from school and we had to make new friends. We still looked out for IL (Fermanagh) registered cars, or ones with Topping's labels on the back windows, or lorries heading for the Scottish Wholesale Society. Getting from Portadown to Bundoran now involved using the 11.15 am from Belfast and travelling via Omagh to Bundoran Junction. This re-introduced us to the Fintona horse tram. We had seen it before on journeys to Donegal, or on a journey to England in 1952, but now it became part of the regular holiday travels. I remember seeing Dick (the horse) only once. Usually, he was safely in the small stable beside the signal cabin, in accordance with the rules. Sight of the tram was, for the mercenary amongst us, the signal to finally open the packet of custard creams!

Changing at Bundoran Junction at Eastertime, from the Omagh direction, now meant facing that footbridge with suitcases on our way *to* Bundoran, the reverse of what happened when we started at Enniskillen. Summer travel should have been easier, using one of the Belfast to Bundoran through coaches. Unfortunately the through coach on the 11.15 am was usually full by Portadown and we had to change trains in the usual fashion anyway, but this had one compensation. We had seldom encountered Jimmy Kelly on the Bundoran branch but in those final summers of '56 and '57 we travelled behind him between Omagh and the Junction. My mother missed Enniskillen and all her friends there and I remember her having a long chat with Jimmy at the Junction. Probably because I wasn't in the through coach, I have no recollection of the shunt being done at the Junction. Of all my journeys on the branch, I can remember noticing the engine number only once and that was on the final run to Bundoran. The number was 74 and I remember deliberately studying the colours and shading of the numerals on the glistening black cabside.

After the line closed in 1957, we continued to travel to Bundoran by train as far as Omagh where we boarded UTA buses for the rest of the journey. It was melancholic, to say the least, to see the line lying intact in so many places especially at Omagh where the running lines were downgraded to sidings. It was on one of those journeys to Bundoran that I stepped off the bus, in Kesh of all places, to post a letter to the Transport Museum to buy my first-ever railway book — Morton's *Standard Gauge Railways in the North of Ireland*.

It was some years before the lifting trains began to run and, even then, they ran in Northern Ireland only. Both Bundoran and Ballyshannon were left more or less intact long after the lifting train had finally reached Omagh in 1962. This was something of a blessing in disguise for my brother and I, as we could explore Bundoran station to our hearts' content. We were able to move the turntable and even use the metal name-printing machine in the summer of 1962! In 1964, we were still able to buy GN-printed tickets from Portadown to Bundoran. On the way home I managed to hold on to the return half. But when I told my mother what I had done, she insisted that I go back to the barrier and give it to the ticket collector, Mr Robinson, as she did not want him to get into trouble!

About this time, too, the Railway Bar in Bundoran sported a new illuminated sign. It was a three-quarter view of a CIE A class MetroVick! It made me wonder, not for the first time, whether such machines would still be running through Bundoran if the coastal route to Sligo had ever been built. It is not beyond the bounds of possibility that such a line would still be open to-day, perhaps as far as Ballyshannon!

In the summer of 1965, after the Derry Road had closed, the bus journey began at Portadown station. It was to be my last journey by public transport to Bundoran. I travelled on the Saturday before 12 July and there were so many people that extra buses were hastily summoned. I got a seat right at the front of one of them, a front-entrance vehicle. Then the driver got in and asked "Does anyone know the road to Enniskillen?" I had a job for the morning! During the break in Enniskillen, I headed for the Melvin Cafe which had been our favourite place for ice-cream, though Shaw's in Belmore Street came a close second. Sadly, I didn't see Bridie Pope, who used to preside in the shop, nor did the ice-cream have the distinctive hint of lemon and 'something else' that I remembered so fondly. I have no idea what that 'something else' was; only once have I found something close. That was in northern Italy another seven years later — while photographing steam trains, of course!

Another very late remembrance of Enniskillen came in August 1970 when I had my last trip in Railcar B, by then belonging to Coras Iompair Eireann and renumbered 2509. It worked in various places on the CIE system after they bought it and I even managed to photograph it at Portadown in December 1964, while it was being used to familiarise CIE drivers with the GNR main line north of Dundalk. In 1970 it was working in the Rosslare area. A party of us from the north joined an Irish Railway Record Society trip from Rosslare across the South Wexford line to Waterford and then over the goods-only Ballinacourty branch before returning to Waterford. For me it was a splendid farewell to a well-remembered car. The weather was great, the photography was good and the car ran well, even if the gear changing gave some problems. Some of us rode in the driver's cab on the way back from Ballinacourty (it was at the trailing end) and we topped 44 mph a couple of times. The saloon windows in 'B' caught a few people out, though. In most coaches with sliding toplights, you slide a small pane away on each side of the centre to reveal the opening. In Railcar B, though, the opposite applies; the movable panes and openings are in the top right and top left corners of the window. On quite a few occasions on that trip, we saw folk attempt to look out by flinging the toplights apart only to collide violently with the permanent glass beyond! Railcar 2509 has been preserved, but is now in almost derelict condition. At the time of writing, plans are being made to have her moved to a site in Fermanagh and, one hopes, restore her to her full glory. Consider yourself heartily encouraged to help!

Another Sligo Leitrim vehicle in preservation is, of course, the locomotive *Lough Erne*, now in the care of the Railway Preservation Society of Ireland at Whitehead. My brother and I had photographed it many times in its UTA and NIR days around Belfast and as we have been involved with the RPSI almost since its inception, have worked on the loco at Whitehead. Naturally we both have a soft spot for an engine going back so far into our roots. John was the fireman when the engine was steamed for what turned out to be its last boiler inspection, in April 1971. On that occasion, it took many hours of hard work and gentle persuasion to bring the steam pressure up to blowing off. John even resorted to emptying the ashpan in an attempt to get the engine to make steam! Later that month *Lough Erne* carried the Governor of Northern Ireland, Lord Grey, when he visited Whitehead — he was supposed to ride in the brakevan behind, but chose the footplate instead!

So far as I can make out, *Lough Erne* was last used on 8 July 1971 on the Society's Summer Train Rides at the Whitehead site. Since then it has been a static exhibit, needing a lot of money to restore it to full health. One Fermanagh enthusiast, George Stevenson, made a great job of repainting the engine on his visits to Whitehead, before his untimely death.

The Enniskillen wheel turned again in 1986. A friend of mine, Rev John McKegney, was on Ulster Television's advisory panel. During a visit to Fermanagh, the District Council entertained them to afternoon tea in the newly-opened Ardhowen Theatre. John was gazing at the splendid view of the remains of the Weirs Bridge when Gerry Burns, the Council's Chief Executive, passed a comment that it would be great to relive the days of the railway. John, who knew of my connections with Enniskillen, said "I know just the man…" The upshot was that I was asked to present the first of (so far) four highly enjoyable railway nights in the Ardhowen. Without John's prompting, a whole cycle of things might not have happened, including this book! The saying about oaks and little acorns is apt, since John is a Derry man.

I hope you enjoy this book as much as I have enjoyed reliving my childhood while compiling it.

THE HISTORY OF FERMANAGH'S RAILWAYS

Norman Johnston

Having set the scene with a personal touch from each of us, it is now appropriate to look in more detail at Fermanagh's railways. We have defined 'Fermanagh' somewhat liberally in this book, rather than stopping dead at the county boundary. Thus the photographic section begins at Clones, an important junction, which was the entry point to Fermanagh for trains from County Monaghan. Likewise Bundoran Junction was, strictly speaking, in County Tyrone, as was Fivemiletown on the Clogher Valley Railway. The Bundoran branch presented a particular problem as it crisscrossed several times between Fermanagh and Donegal. In the end we decided to include the whole branch since it would make no sense to exclude Pettigo, Ballyshannon and Bundoran. After all, Pettigo served the County Fermanagh hamlet of Tullyhommon and Bundoran was the natural holiday destination for Fermanagh folk.

In the 1950s Fermanagh was associated with two railways — the Sligo Leitrim and Northern Counties Railway (SLNCR) and the Great Northern Railway (Ireland). However, the GNR was itself an amalgam of a number of earlier railways and at this point we need to give a brief outline of the history of these earlier lines, as they relate to Fermanagh. Enniskillen must have seemed a very desirable destination for Victorian railway builders because no fewer than three companies aimed to reach there. These were the Londonderry and Enniskillen Railway, the Newry and Enniskillen Railway and the Dundalk and Enniskillen Railway, all three of which were incorporated by Act of Parliament in July 1845. At that time the only public transport available to Fermanagh were the daily Bianconi 'long cars', one of which ran by road from Enniskillen to Dublin via Cavan, Virginia and Navan and the other from Sligo to Omagh via Enniskillen. The county was effectively isolated to all but the most hardened and determined traveller.

The Londonderry and Enniskillen Railway

The LER was the first to reach Enniskillen. The aim of the line's promoters was to tap the potential traffic of Tyrone and Fermanagh to the benefit of the port of Derry/Londonderry. The line was surveyed by none other than the famous Robert Stephenson, son of George Stephenson, the designer of the steam locomotive *Rocket* which won the Rainhill trials so convincingly in 1829. The company was financed from London but progress was painfully slow. Although Strabane was reached in 1847, it was to be 1852 before the line reached Omagh. The route from Omagh to Enniskillen was opened in stages, the last stretch — from Dromore Road to Enniskillen — being opened on 19 August 1854. The original LER station in Enniskillen was alongside what is now the Irvinestown Road, just opposite Sedan Terrace and north of where the Pound Brae overbridge used to be (see the photographs on page 74 for a view of the general area). The company's finances were in a poor state from the very beginning and it was heavily in debt. Nevertheless it was enterprising in some respects. It was a shareholder in the Lough Erne Steam Navigation Company which operated a paddle steamer *Countess of Milan* from Enniskillen to Belleek and to Belturbet on alternate days. The LER ran excursions to Enniskillen to connect with these sailings.

The company was plunged into controversy four weeks after it was opened, by the derailment of an Apprentice Boys special at Trillick (Co Tyrone) as it returned from Derry to Enniskillen on 15 September 1854. There were fatalities, and accusations that the derailment was malicious. A number of permanent way men were tried in Omagh but were eventually acquitted for lack of evidence. Trouble in the 'marching season' is nothing new!

The Londonderry and Enniskillen Railway remained isolated from the rest of the railway system until 1859 when the Dundalk and Enniskillen Railway arrived. A year later the LER was leased to the DER with effect from 1 January 1860. This meant that the LER received a guaranteed income from the lease, the DER taking responsibility for running the line and making a profit or loss as the case may be. This lease was taken over by the GNR when it was formed in 1876. The LER remained a separate company until it was bought out by the GNR in 1883.

The Dundalk and Enniskillen Railway

The other two companies which aimed to reach Enniskillen were the Dundalk and Enniskillen Railway and the Newry and Enniskillen Railway. The latter company was to connect the port of Newry to Enniskillen by way of Markethill, Armagh, Monaghan and Clones. The Dundalk and Enniskillen Railway was to connect Dundalk with Clones and to share the responsibility and cost of the remaining 22 miles with the NER. In the event, the NER got no further than Armagh and even that took until 1864! Accepting the inevitable, the company formally abandoned plans to build beyond Armagh in 1857 and renamed itself the Newry and Armagh Railway. The Ulster Railway had already obtained powers to build the Armagh to Clones section, and the DER took full responsibility for the Clones to Enniskillen section.

The Dundalk and Enniskillen Railway, meanwhile, had been constructing its line from Dundalk and had reached Newbliss in 1855. Progress over the next two years was slow and the Newbliss-Clones-Lisnaskea section was not opened until 7 July 1858. Lisnaskea was a temporary terminus for six weeks, the section to Lisbellaw opening on 16 August. Six months later, Enniskillen saw its first train from Clones on 15 February 1859. The station was the later GNR one, at Forthill, roughly where the car park is now. Steps were quickly taken to connect with the LER station. The connecting line was on a 330 ft radius curve which was the tightest on the whole GNR system. The curve took the line through 90° in 200 yds, from the DER station to the LER one, not counting the 60° already negotiated, as the Clones line entered the station. Because of the curve's severity there was a five miles per hour restriction over it. There is some evidence that the DER was allowed to use the LER station until their own was completed. Shortly after the LER line was leased, Lord Erne (a major shareholder in the LER) said in March 1860 that he wanted trains from Omagh "to stop only at the Dundalk station". The LER station closed soon afterwards and in later years the 'Derry cattle beach' was the only surviving relic of the old station.

From 1860 the Dundalk-Enniskillen-Derry line was operated as one concern, a main line of 121½ miles. In view of its increased responsibilities, the name of the company was changed on 7 July 1862 to the Irish North Western Railway. Although this name only lasted until the formation of the GNR in 1876, the route through Fermanagh was always referred to by railwaymen as 'The Irish North'.

The Belfast connection

The 'Irish North' in 1860 offered Fermanagh residents easy access to both Derry and Dublin (then the capital of the whole island), but as yet the 'Irish North' had connections only at its extremities. To get from Enniskillen to Belfast by rail involved a 62 mile journey to Dundalk and a further 58 miles via the Dublin and Belfast Junction Railway (DBJR) and the Ulster Railway. The Ulster Railway from Belfast had reached Armagh in 1848 and Monaghan in 1858, so a more sensible route from Enniskillen to Belfast, at this time, was 22 miles by rail Enniskillen to Clones (which was not yet a junction), 12 miles by road Clones to Monaghan and 53 miles by rail Monaghan to Belfast.

However the Ulster Railway had plans to provide connections to the 'Irish North' at both Clones and Omagh. First to come was the Omagh connection. The Portadown and Dungannon Junction Railway (worked by the UR) opened in 1858 and, renaming itself the Portadown, Dungannon and Omagh Junction Railway, extended to Omagh in September 1861. From that point Omagh became the most sensible route from Enniskillen to Belfast. Six months later Clones also became a junction when the Clones and Cavan Extension Railway opened on 7 April 1862. This line was financed by four companies (Dublin and Drogheda Railway, DBJR, UR and INWR) but was worked by the INWR (strictly speaking still called the DER until July 1862). The Cavan line made a head-on connection with the Midland Great Western Railway's Cavan branch, thus providing an alternative route to Dublin. Finally, on 2 March 1863, the Ulster

Railway opened through to Clones, providing a second connection to Belfast and turning Clones into a railway crossroads. At Clones, the UR built its own engine shed and goods yard, which were just off Rosslea Street, adjacent to the junction with the Dundalk line. The INWR shed was on the site of the later GNR roundhouse shed which replaced both sheds in 1924.

The Bundoran branch.

Around 1860 plans were being formulated to build a railway through north Fermanagh to Bundoran. In July 1861 the Enniskillen and Bundoran Railway was incorporated with powers to build a 35 mile line from the LER near Lowtherstown (as Irvinestown was then called) to Bundoran. A year later, in June 1862, this scheme was modified to include an extension to Sligo (23 miles further on) and the company was renamed the Enniskillen, Bundoran and Sligo Railway (EBSR). If this had been built in its entirety, it is much less likely than the Sligo Leitrim line would have been built later. At Sligo the EBSR would have linked up with the north western terminus of the MGWR. The INWR had a significant financial stake in the EBSR and worked the Bundoran line from its opening on 13 June 1866. The plan to extend to Sligo never came to anything and was finally killed off by the opening of the SLNCR in 1881. The Bundoran line had a junction with the INWR at a point between Ballinamallard and Trillick, close to what is now the village of Kilskeery. The junction was initially known as Lowtherstown Road. As Bundoran increased in importance as a holiday resort, the junction was renamed Bundoran Junction, and was one of only a few triangular junctions in Ireland, the layout providing for through running to Bundoran from both Enniskillen and Omagh. Lowtherstown was owned by the D'Arcy Irvines and, shortly after the railway was built, they had its name changed to Irvinestown. Despite the extensive mileage of railway which it now operated, the INWR suffered from the sparse population and comparative poverty in the area that it served. There was little or no industry except in Dundalk and Derry and, in mid-Victorian times, few people had money to spare for leisure travel. The INWR was unable to pay any dividends to its shareholders after 1862. From 1874 the line began to make a loss. It was with some relief that the proprietors of the INWR welcomed the formation of the GNR in 1876.

The Great Northern Railway (Ireland)

The impetus for the creation of the Great Northern Railway stemmed from the fact that the line between Belfast and Dublin was operated by three different companies — the Dublin and Drogheda Railway, the Dublin and Belfast Junction Railway (Drogheda to Portadown) and the Ulster Railway (Portadown to Belfast). Amalgamation would reduce journey times and bring greater efficiency and thus greater profit. It also seemed sensible to bring the INWR into any such amalgamation, to develop traffic between west Ulster and Dublin and Belfast. However the main obstacle was that the highly profitable Ulster Railway valued its independence too much and the equally profitable DDR did not want to proceed without it. An attempt in 1868 failed to reach agreement but, in the end, the DDR decided to proceed anyway. On 1 March 1875 it amalgamated with the DBJR to form the Northern Railway which, on 1 January 1876, was joined by the INWR. The weaker companies had to join on less favourable terms and the loss-making INWR found its shares devalued from £30 to £5 in the process. These moves made the UR look more seriously at amalgamation and so it was that on 1 April 1876 it joined the new combine, the enlarged company adopting the title Great Northern Railway (Ireland). The word 'Ireland' was added to distinguish the company from the already established Great Northern Railway in England.

The creation of the GNR had little immediate impact in Fermanagh, as all the existing railways there were operated by one company in any case. However, gradually the new organisation made itself felt with new locomotives and rolling stock and the loss-making lines in Fermanagh were to some extent subsidised by profit from the other lines. The GNR certainly developed traffic on the Bundoran line, which it purchased from the EBSR in 1897. In 1899 it bought and modernised an hotel in Bundoran, renaming it the Great Northern Hotel.

The Sligo Leitrim

In 1877 a new railway began to become part of the railway scene in Fermanagh. A link between Enniskillen and Sligo had long been on the cards. At one time the LER had considered extending to Sligo, and of course the EBSR had similar plans. Sligo itself had been reached from Dublin by the Midland Great Western Railway in December 1862. The impetus for building the Sligo Leitrim and Northern Counties Railway came from the landowners and prosperous farmers of Sligo and Leitrim. In the late nineteenth century there was a growing trade in the export of live cattle from Ireland to England to provide beef, and the farmers of this region needed a railway to transport cattle to the docks at Dublin, Belfast and Derry. The 42 mile line was authorised by Act of Parliament in 1875 and its promoters planned a route from Enniskillen (where there was a junction with the GNR) via Florencecourt, Belcoo, Manorhamilton and Dromahair to a junction with the MGWR near Collooney some five miles from Sligo (though with running rights into Sligo).

Construction began in 1877 at the Enniskillen end, the first section — from Enniskillen to Belcoo — opening to goods traffic on 12 February 1879, and to passengers on 18 March. The line was extended by degrees to Glenfarne (1 January 1880), Manorhamilton (1 December 1880) and Collooney (1 September 1881). The junction with the MGWR at Collooney was not finally completed until 7 November 1882, after which through running between Enniskillen and Sligo became possible.

The SLNCR was never a prosperous company and ran its line very much on a shoestring. Its staple traffic was live cattle and it certainly carried far more bovine than human passengers. The opening of the SLNCR greatly increased the amount of traffic from Enniskillen on the GNR. Enniskillen became a staging post for the forwarding of live cattle to Derry and Belfast from the farms of Leitrim, Sligo and even further afield. All this kept the 'Sligo yard' at Enniskillen very busy with constant shunting and transfer of cattle wagons. The SLNCR locomotives were a common sight in Enniskillen and added to the rich variety of locomotives to be seen.

Unusually, if not uniquely, SLNCR locomotives carried names but not numbers, a practice more common on early Victorian railways or on industrial systems. After the withdrawal of the last ex-GNR 0-6-0 tender locomotives in 1949, all the locomotives were 0-6-4Ts, an unusual wheel arrangement. There were three varieties of these — *Fermanagh, Leitrim, Lurganboy, Lissadell* and *Hazlewood* dating from 1882-99, *Sir Henry, Enniskillen* and *Lough Gill* dating from 1904-17, and *Lough Melvin* and *Lough Erne* from 1949 (though not delivered until 1951 as the company could not pay for them, and eventually resorted to a hire purchase deal). Like other lines operating on shoe-string finances, the SLNCR was one of the first to experiment with diesel traction for passenger traffic. From 1935 a railbus was operated and a second added in 1938. These handled all the passenger traffic except a daily mixed steam train. In 1947 the SLNCR purchased a much more substantial articulated diesel railcar from Walkers of Wigan which, with one railbus, operated the passenger service until closure. This railcar still exists and there are tentative plans to try and have it returned to Fermanagh.

The Clogher Valley Railway

The last railway to be built in Fermanagh was the Clogher Valley Railway, the only narrow gauge line to operate in the county. It was built to serve the prosperous mixed farming area of the Clogher Valley and ran through a scenic and attractive hinterland. To visitors, the term 'Clogher Valley' seems a bit of a misnomer as it is not that evidently a valley. However, to the north is a range of low mountains which includes Cloghtogle, Topped, Brougher, Ballyness, Knockmany and Slievemore, whilst some four or five miles to the south is another range which includes Slieve Beagh, Essrawer and Culla More. Between these two ranges is the valley shared by the Colebrook River flowing south west and the Blackwater, flowing north east. The Clogher Valley contains no major towns, but rather a string of small ones. From west to east these are

Brookeborough, Fivemiletown, Clogher, Augher and Ballygawley. The purpose of the railway was to link both ends of the valley to the GNR system in a 37 mile line which had no branches. Starting at Maguiresbridge (on the Enniskillen to Clones line) it went to Brookeborough and hence the other villages listed above, leaving the valley at Ballygawley to climb steeply south towards Aughnacloy and Caledon, before rejoining the GNR at Tynan, on the Clones to Portadown line.

The Clogher Valley Railway was essentially a 3'0" gauge roadside steam tramway. It was incorporated by Act of Council in May 1884, under the terms of the Tramway and Public Companies Act of 1883, which allowed any losses incurred in operating the tramway to be made good by the local ratepayers under 'baronial guarantee'. Initially known as the Clogher Valley Tramway, the line was opened on 2 May 1887. Seven years later, in 1894, the company renamed itself the Clogher Valley Railway, the new name carrying more dignity, it appeared, than 'tramway'. At Maguiresbridge, where the line crossed the road to Lisnaskea, pedestrians waiting at the crossing sometimes asked "When's the tram coming?" to which the crossing keeper would reply irritably, "It's not a tram, it's a train!"

Although the railway followed the public road for most of its length, it had its own trackbed in several places where steep gradients had to be avoided. The most significant of these was a three mile stretch near Maguiresbridge, over what was known locally as 'the Commons', but there were other stretches at Clogher and on either side of Aughnacloy. These perhaps justified the title 'railway' though, on the other hand, at Fivemiletown, Augher and Caledon the CVR trains went along the centre of the main street, a fact which in the 1930s led to congestion and blockages as the number of cars grew.

The majority of passenger trains consisted of a bogie carriage and brake van, hauled by a small tramway type 0-4-2T with side skirts and cow-catcher, running cab first. Some trains ran only between Tynan and Fivemiletown, the Fermanagh end of the line attracting much less traffic. Like the SLNCR, the CVR went over to diesel traction in the 1930s. In 1932 it acquired a Gardner-engined articulated railcar, seating 28, the first of its kind in these islands, if not in the world. The CVR also purchased an additional unit, termed a diesel 'tractor' with no passenger portion. This unit was fitted with a lorry type body, rather like a five plank wagon. It sometimes ran in passenger service hauling a standard coach and brake van. When the line closed in 1941 the County Donegal Railway acquired the railcar, which became No 10 in their fleet. In this form it is now preserved at the Ulster Folk and Transport Museum, Cultra.

The Clogher Valley Railway was largely a Tyrone railway. Only the first eight miles or so were in Fermanagh, and, apart from Maguiresbridge, the only stations in Fermanagh were Brookeborough and Colebrook, the latter station serving Colebrook Estate, owned by Lord Brookborough. After crossing the county boundary into Tyrone near Fivemiletown, the railway remained in Tyrone, apart from the last mile or so, when it crossed into Co Armagh to terminate at Tynan. Between Ballygawley and

The Clogher Valley Railway railcar at Aughnacloy on 25 June 1937, in company with brake van No 5. The railcar was numbered 'No 1' and could seat 28. It was built by Walker Bros of Wigan in December 1932 and had a Gardner six-cylinder 6LZ diesel engine. For economy, the rear bogie was second hand from a CVR coach!

Tynan it virtually hugged the border with Co Monaghan, but at no time crossed into it, thus avoiding the need for customs stops after partition in 1921.

The CVR stations were very distinctive, consisting of single storey red brick buildings, one end of which usually had a short upper storey. They were ornamented with attractive barge boards and coping tiles, and all still survive in some form or other. Brookeborough station has recently been restored as a cross-community project, with

'The Unit', otherwise known as 'No 2'. The lorry body was removable, so it could double as a spare power unit for the railcar. Note the crude repair to the side sheet over the wheels, following an argument with Brookeborough level crossing gates!

part of the building used by a play group. The platform has been reflagged and a length of track is to be laid. Rather oddly the CVR had no buildings at either Maguiresbridge or Tynan, the GNR facilities there being used by passengers. The company headquarters and workshop facilities were at Aughnacloy, near the eastern end of the line.

Into the Twentieth Century

In terms of construction, the Fermanagh railway map was complete by 1887 and for the next forty years or so the railways had no significant rivals for the provision of transport. Even when motor cars began to appear after 1900, there were relatively few in Fermanagh, apart from those owned by doctors and the wealthy. The state of the roads and the distance to Belfast and Dublin meant that the few cars which existed were largely used for local journeys. The GNR trains used in Fermanagh gradually modernised. In 1876, when the GNR was formed, the passenger trains were made up of a mixture of four and six-wheel carriages, hauled by 2-4-0 locomotives, with some 2-2-2s and the last of the old LER light 2-2-0WTs. By the early 1900s most trains consisted of six-wheelers, and after the First World War, bogie carriages began to appear. By the late 1920s the majority of trains had corridor coaches. The Fermanagh lines were regarded as secondary routes by the GNR management, so the carriages used on them were ones that had been built for the main lines 15-20 years earlier. For example, carriages used on main line expresses in 1900-1905, might find their way to Fermanagh in 1915-25.

In contrast, the steep grades on some of the 'Irish North' lines led to specific engines being designed for them. The first 4-4-0 locomotives built for the GNR, in 1885, were designed for the 'Irish North', and had 5'7" driving wheels. All subsequent GNR passenger tender locomotives were 4-4-0s, but most of them had 6'7" wheels. Other engines designed with the 'Irish North' in mind were the P5'6" class in 1892-5 (added to in 1904-5) and the U class, introduced in 1915, which had 5'9" wheels and were known as the 'Irish North engines'. In contrast to the small passenger engines used, the Fermanagh lines of the GNR carried heavy goods traffic and justified the use of some of the largest goods engines the company possessed. These included engines in power categories 'C' an 'D'.

Between the Wars

The period immediately before the First World War can justifiably be described as the heyday of railways all over the British Isles. After the war the financial position of Irish railways deteriorated considerably. Some of the reasons for this were shared by railways elsewhere. The introduction of the eight hour day in 1919 led to rising wage costs, as hours over the eight had to be paid at overtime rates. Trade Union power resulted in a rise in the level of wages generally. This was no bad thing if you were a railway worker, but affected the ability of the railways to remain profitable. Ireland had a lower density of traffic than most English railways, which made it particularly difficult to cover operating costs. On the GNR the reality was that the main Belfast-Dublin line was profitable and largely subsidised less economic lines such as those in Fermanagh.

The GNR was further affected by the partition of Ireland in 1921. The creation of Northern Ireland and the Irish Free State affected three lines which each crossed the new international border only once — the SLNCR, the Londonderry and Lough Swilly Railway, and the Dundalk, Newry and Greenore Railway, and one which crossed it twice — the County Donegal Railway. None were disadvantaged like the GNR which crossed the new international border no fewer than 15 times, 10 of these on the Fermanagh border alone. Six of the crossings were between Clones and Cavan but, since there were no stations north of the border on this line, they were disregarded and the line operated as if it were entirely within the Irish Free State. Much more significant was the crossing on the Clones-Enniskillen line which required customs examination at Clones (IFS) and Newtownbutler (NI). Similarly the Bundoran branch crossed into Co Donegal briefly at Pettigo, returning to Fermanagh as far as Belleek, after which it again entered the Free State. There were therefore customs stops at Kesh (NI), Pettigo (IFS), Belleek (NI) and Ballyshannon (IFS). This greatly added to journey times. Travellers between Portadown and Fermanagh faced additional customs stops at Tynan (NI) and Glaslough (IFS) on the Portadown-Clones line.

Apart from the inconvenience to travellers, the border affected the pattern of freight traffic in the long term. Traffic north of the border gradually tended to gravitate towards Belfast and south of the border towards Dublin. Towns on the border itself were affected by changing shopping patterns. Clones, once a thriving town commercially, declined in later years to the advantage of Cavan and Monaghan, and Lisnaskea — a mere village in the 1950s — is now bigger than Clones.

The partition of Ireland also had an impact on the way railway transport was organised. In Britain the government forced the various railway companies to amalgamate into four large companies (the Grouping) in 1923. This was mirrored in the Irish Free State when all railways exclusively within the Free State were amalgamated into the Great Southern Railways in 1925. This amalgamation did not involve the five companies which had lines crossing the border. Within Northern Ireland there was no parallel move, as the only two railways of any significance, which did not cross the border, were the Northern Counties Committee (owned by the LMS in Britain) and the Belfast and County Down Railway. There was little point in amalgamating just these two, since the GNR operated as big a mileage in the North as both put together. The attitude of the Northern Unionist government was not very favourable to the GNR. With its headquarters and management in a 'rival' state, the GNR was viewed with some suspicion, if not hostility.

Enter the buses

Into this volatile situation a further complication appeared in the 1920s in the shape of bus competition. In looking at this we will focus on Fermanagh, but the problem was universal, affecting all railway companies. The first bus operator in Fermanagh was Hezekiah Appleby who, in February 1926, formed the 'Central Omnibus Company in direct competition with the Sligo Leitrim. He ran a twice daily bus between Enniskillen and Sligo, charging 5/= (25p) single and 7/6 (37.5p) return. Appleby was actually married to a cousin of my mother's, Jenny Connolly. He was known as 'Hez' for short and was a fun-loving character. In 1929 he started a second route, this time from Enniskillen to Bundoran by Belcoo. This ran only in the summer months, and aimed to siphon off some of the GNR's Bundoran branch traffic. A second operator appeared in 1926 when Captain Merrilies and his son in law William Clarke began an Enniskillen to

Derrygonnelly service, adding a route to Derrylin in 1927. These did not directly compete with train services. By 1927 Clarke had taken over the operation and, as Clarke's *Blue Bus Services*, extended to Fivemiletown and Rosslea and even began a service to Lough Derg for the local pilgrims. This was the main destination of the GNR's 'Bundoran Express' which brought pilgrims, mainly from the Irish Free State.

In 1927 a potentially much more serious competitor entered the field when the largest bus company in Ulster, the newly formed 'Belfast Omnibus Company' (BOC), began a Belfast to Enniskillen service routed through the Clogher Valley. The service had three trips daily and undercut the GNR fare. However, at 4 hours 15 mins for the 93 mile trip, it took considerably longer than the train, so passengers travelled on it if cost was more significant than speed or comfort. The BOC in fact posed more of a threat to the CVR against which it could also compete on speed. Indeed, it opened a bus depot in Fivemiletown. The other early bus operators in Fermanagh can be summarised as follows:

Hard Rocks Motor Service, Lisbellaw, owned by E W McCreary. It operated two buses on an Enniskillen-Tempo service. It also worked to Bundoran in the summer. McCreary was bought out by Clarke in 1933. *Fleetwing Bus Service*, Omagh, owned by W A Simpson. It ran a service between Omagh and Enniskillen from November 1927, competing with the GNR. By 1934 there were four trips daily, two via Trillick and two via Irvinestown. *Dreadnought Motor Service*, Omagh, owned by C H Donaghy. It began to compete with Simpson in 1928, but was bought out by the GNR in 1931. Phair Brothers of Belturbet (Co Cavan) ran a service to Enniskillen, via Swanlinbar, twice daily. They too were bought out by the GNR. W E White, in 1928-9, operated a bus from Enniskillen to Longford, via Swanlinbar, with two trips daily. His operation ended abruptly in August 1929 when his bus was wrecked in an accident.

The most enduring of the early operators was Maurice Cassidy who, in 1929, started the 'Erne Bus Service'. His familiar brown and cream buses were to be a feature of Fermanagh's roads up to the early 1960s. Cassidy's main routes were Enniskillen-Clones (five workings), and Enniskillen-Belleek-Bundoran, but he also worked to Rosslea and ran as far afield as Clones-Cavan and Clones-Cootehill. By the mid-1930s he had five buses, (see pages 138-141).

The Northern Ireland Road Transport Board

While all this competition was developing, the Northern Ireland government was coming under strong pressure, particularly from the railways, to bring some order and regulation to the chaos. The railways saw potential in buses as feeders to the railways, but did not want them duplicating their services. The GNR, NCC and BCDR had all adopted a policy of buying out their competitors, Donaghy and Phair Bros being cases in point.

Parallel to the development of bus services, private operators began to purchase lorries and compete with the railways for goods traffic. They managed quite often to capture the more profitable elements of the freight business, leaving the bulkier and less economic traffic to the trains. By 1934 it was estimated that in Northern Ireland more goods were being carried by road than by rail.

In 1934, the Northern Ireland government set up a committee of inquiry into road and rail transport chaired by Sir Felix Pole, a retired manager of the Great Western Railway in Britain. As a result of Pole's report, the Road and Rail Traffic Act (NI) 1935 was passed. This implemented the report's main recommendation by setting up the Northern Ireland Road Transport Board (NIRTB), which was given powers to establish a monopoly for the operation of all bus and road freight services within Northern Ireland. Over the next year or so all private operators operating entirely within Northern Ireland were obliged to sell out to the NIRTB. This included the Omagh based Fleetwood Bus Service, and Clarke's Blue Bus Services, as well as the BOC, which was the core of the new company. Those operators with cross-border routes had to relinquish the Northern Ireland portion of their routes. Thus Hez Appleby had to give up two of his four buses in 1937, and confine himself to the Sligo-Blacklion part of his route. In 1945 Appleby sold his remaining two buses to the SLNCR (see pages 136-7). One odd anomaly was that the Erne

Bus Service managed to retain its independence, mainly due to the extent of its cross-border operations.

The railways, which by this time were extensive bus and lorry operators in their own right, had to give up those portions of their fleets which operated within Northern Ireland. The GNR lost 50 of its 171 buses and 126 of its 153 lorries. The NCC and BCDR, being entirely within Northern Ireland, lost their entire fleets. The GNR was able to retain some services which originated in the Free State but terminated north of the border. The companies were compensated with NIRTB shares, but the promised coordination of road and rail was not fulfilled. By the late 1930s the railways in Fermanagh were facing competition from a more efficient and ruthless NIRTB, which now had a major depot in Enniskillen. Worse still, from the railways' point of view, the success of the NIRTB had the effect of convincing the Northern Ireland government that buses and lorries provided a cheap and efficient solution to the province's public transport needs. This resulted in a mind set which, after the war, was unwilling to invest public money in the railways and preferred instead to close them.

Lacking the short branch lines which featured in some areas, the Fermanagh railways avoided any actual closures until 1957, but the CVR, vulnerable to bus competition because of its slow speed, closed for good on 31 December 1941, even its diesel railcar being unable to save it.

The War Years

By 1939, many railways, but particularly the GNR, were facing a bleak future and closures seemed inevitable. Traffic was declining, costs were rising and, as private companies, the railways were not subsidised in any way. Long term prospects were poor as car ownership was rising and roads improving (at public expense) to the advantage of buses and other road users. From this perspective the outbreak of war saved the railways from imminent crisis. Petrol rationing drove private transport off the roads, whilst the needs of war vastly increased traffic on the railways and returned them to profitability. On the GNR the number of passengers carried annually increased from 5 million in 1939 to nearly 11 million by 1944. Goods tonnage increased from about ¾ million tons in 1939 to 1¼ million tons in 1944. Fermanagh played a significant part in the war with the big flying boat base at Castle Archdale and other air bases at St Angelo and Killadeas. These and other military movements required regular troop trains to Fermanagh, routed via Omagh (to avoid violating the Free State's neutrality). The demand for fresh food for Britain benefited not only Fermanagh farmers, but also those south of the border who dispatched their produce by the Sligo Leitrim, as well as the GNR.

The war had some interesting effects on the cross-border trains of the GNR. The UK during the war operated on double summer time to maximise daylight hours for production, whilst the Free State used ordinary summer time. The Bundoran branch timetable had to show British time at the Fermanagh stations, but Free State time at Pettigo, Ballyshannon and Bundoran. This gave the impression that Down trains were taking 45 minutes from Bundoran Junction to Bundoran whilst the Up trains took 2 hours 45 minutes! A train could leave Kesh at 8.31 pm and arrive at Pettigo at 7.41 pm!

Before leaving the war years, I must tell a story which I heard recently from an old soldier who had served in the British Army of the Rhine in the late 1940s. It is a well known fact that Nazi Germany had plans in 1940 to invade Ireland, including Northern Ireland. When the soldier arrived in Germany in 1946, his unit were issued with maps to help them find their way about. These were printed on the back of maps originally issued to the German army. His turned out to be a German map of Ulster, showing the proposed route for an invasion. The plan appeared to involve landing at Bundoran and approaching Belfast from the west. Rail transport for soldiers and tanks was a vital part of this plan, but whatever spies the Germans used clearly did not penetrate Fermanagh or Tyrone, because the map showed the Clogher Valley Railway as a major rail artery across south Ulster. The image of the Wehrmacht arriving at Maguiresbridge to requisition ten troop trains and use of the CVR tank transporters is an amusing one!

After the War 1945-53

The end of the Second World War in 1945 did not bring an immediate return to the prewar financial crisis. Although rather run down, the railways were in a strong position because of continued petrol rationing and the difficulty in obtaining new cars, which persisted until about 1950. Profit made during the war allowed the GNR to purchase 15 new steam locomotives in 1947-8. Five of these were a new batch of U class 4-4-0s, Nos 201-205, which were finished in sky blue livery and named *Meath, Louth, Armagh, Antrim* and *Down* respectively. They were unusual in having rectangular windows in the cab sides instead of the usual curved cut outs. They were regulars on the Bundoran Express and other Fermanagh trains. They were also the first blue engines in Fermanagh, and the first named GNR engines in Fermanagh since the period of the First World War. They were soon complemented by the 1915 batch (196-200) which were painted blue as they went through works and also given names — *Lough Gill, Lough Neagh, Lough Swilly, Lough Derg* and *Lough Melvin*. These ten engines, though not confined to Fermanagh, added much needed colour to the trains of the county over the next ten years. In 1950 the GNR also purchased ten three-coach diesel trains which were the first of their type in either Britain or Ireland. Each train had two power cars with an unpowered intermediate. One of the new trains was used to operate a direct Belfast-Enniskillen diesel service, via Clones, from 1953.

GNR No 203 *Armagh,* one of the five new U class 4-4-0s built by Beyer Peacock in 1948 and, oddly, the least photographed of this class.

The UTA

Meanwhile railways in general were facing a new phase of reorganisation. In Britain the 'big four' were nationalised in 1948 to create British Railways. This was mirrored in the Irish Free State by the creation of Coras Iompair Eireann in 1945 and its nationalisation three years later. CIE controlled all rail and road transport, including Dublin buses and trams. Following this trend, the Northern Ireland government, in 1948, created the Ulster Transport Authority and brought the BCDR, NCC and NIRTB (though not Belfast Corporation Transport) all under one management. However this left the GNR and the other four cross-border railways out in the cold with an uncertain future.

The UTA reflected the government's attitude towards railways by pruning their railway network drastically in 1950. The remaining lines were dieselised fairly cheaply in the 1950s by rebuilding existing coaches as diesel railcars, with a minimum of new build. In contrast, the 1950s saw considerable investment in new buses with front entrances and in road improvements.

The Great Northern Railway Board

Meanwhile the GNR struggled on as an independent company with no prospect of remaining profitable and no resources to modernise. The crisis point was reached in late 1950, after the company had made a loss over the previous financial year. In January 1951 the GNR announced its intention to close the system and served notice on its employees. Faced with the sudden and complete loss of all rail services in the Great Northern's area, the two governments stepped in to negotiate with the company.

The outcome was that, after meeting the company's current deficits as an interim measure, the governments of Northern Ireland and the Irish Republic purchased the GNR for £4.5M, as from 1 September 1953, each paying half the cost. This created the unique situation of the GNR being effectively nationalised, but owned by two separate states. To administer the company, a board was created called the Great Northern Railway Board, with ten members — five nominated by the Republic's Minister for Industry and Commerce and five by the Northern Minister for Commerce. The chairmanship was rotated annually. This board was responsible for decisions about investment in rolling stock and infrastructure as well as actual operation of the line. It was also charged with meeting operating costs out of revenue as soon as possible. Writing from the vantage point of an age when there is much discussion about the need for cross-border bodies, it is interesting to look at the operation of a cross-border body that existed forty-five years ago!

To the general public there was no visible change, especially as the day to day running of the trains remained with the GNR management. Only the appearance of the word 'Board' in place of 'Ireland' in the company crest and GNRB on cap badges betrayed the new ownership. The main problem faced by the Board was that to meet operating costs out of revenue there had to be investment in new equipment, but that investment had to be agreed and financed by the two governments. In sharing the purchase of the GNR equally the Northern Ireland government got the better part of the bargain, in that more than 50% of the GNR mileage lay within Northern Ireland, but the downside was that it also had to pay 50% of any investment or losses.

Instinctively the Northern Ireland government wanted rid of the GNR as soon as possible. In a period when the two governments rarely communicated with each other about anything, it resented having to cooperate with the Irish Republic over transport policy. The Board wanted to invest over £500,000 in new diesel trains, but it took until mid-1955 before this was approved, and another two years before the first of the new trains was ready. By that time it was just too late to save Fermanagh's railways. Further proposals for new investment met a wall of procrastination and indifference. Essentially the problem stemmed from the differing attitudes of the two governments to transport. The government of the Irish Republic saw railways as an essential part of future transport needs and wanted to invest and save the railways. The Northern Ireland government saw the GNR as an albatross and wanted to save money by replacing trains with buses, except for the Belfast-Dublin main line.

Closure Proposals

Whilst the legislation setting up the GNRB required joint decisions on matters of investment, it also allowed either minister to make unilateral decisions affecting the lines within his specific jurisdiction. Thus the GNR operating management were hostages to fortune after 1953. Decisions about the future of the GNR system could be made without reference to them. This situation allowed the Northern Ireland government to force the closure of certain branch lines inside Northern Ireland in 1955-56 (Banbridge-Scarva, Banbridge-Newcastle, Banbridge-Knockmore Junction, and the Cookstown Branch). Fermanagh was a more difficult proposition as most of its routes were cross-border, and closure ought therefore to have required a joint decision by the two governments. It came as quite a shock therefore when the Northern Ireland government proposed in 1956 that it was going to close the lines from Omagh to Newtownbutler, Portadown to Tynan and Bundoran Junction to Belleek. This proposal was all the more surprising for the people of Fermanagh in that the Prime Minister of Northern Ireland at this time, Lord Brookeborough, was a Fermanagh man.

The proposed closures involved 97¼ route miles, but their knock-on effects would be catastrophic. If the GNR Fermanagh lines closed, the SLNCR, already near the end of its financial resources, would be forced to close— a further 42¾ miles. Similarly the Beleek-Bundoran section could not survive in isolation, likewise Tynan to Monaghan and Newtownbutler to Clones could not remain open — another 22½ miles. It was also unlikely that the GNRB could sustain services on the Cavan-Monaghan and Clones-Dundalk sections once their connections had gone, ultimately affecting yet another 77½ miles. All told therefore these closures were going to eliminate 240 miles of railway line, the largest closures in one sweep up to that time in Ireland.

At meetings of the GNR Board there was deadlock, with the Northern Ireland Chairman recommending complete closure and his counterpart recommending continued financial support. On 5 June 1957 the Northern Ireland government unilaterally told the GNRB that all services on the disputed lines within Northern Ireland were to end on 30 September. Meanwhile the Operating and Civil Engineering departments carried on as if this was not really going to happen. Throughout the summer of 1957, extensive ballasting and relaying was carried out on the Bundoran branch and elsewhere, pointless work if the line was about to close.

The Enniskillen-Belfast Diesel Express

In the spring, the first of the long-awaited new diesel trains was almost ready, and on 19 June the first eight-coach train entered service on the Belfast based 'Enterprise' Belfast-Dublin express. This train had four power cars (701-704) and four non-powered cars. The next train was to be of six cars and was intended for the Belfast-Derry service. However with power car 705 ready but idle, the GNR hit on the idea of using it on a service to Enniskillen to demonstrate the potential of the new trains. Thus it was that on 22 July 1957 a new fast Enniskillen-Belfast service was introduced. The train consisted of power car 705 plus class D³ brake second coach 396, together seating a maximum of 96. The train left Enniskillen at 8.50 am, stopped briefly at Bundoran Junction to connect with the 7.35 am ex-Bundoran, and reached Omagh at 9.35 am. After running round its coach, it left Omagh at 9.45 am and, stopping only at

The Enniskillen-Belfast express approaching Bundoran Junction in August 1957.

Carrickmore to cross a down train, reached Belfast at 11.20 am, thus cutting 65 minutes off the usual schedule.

The return trip left Belfast at 7.00 pm and ran non stop to Omagh (8.26 pm) where it met the 7.00 pm from Derry. It left Omagh at 8.36 pm and ran non-stop to Enniskillen arriving at 9.05 pm. With 2 hours 5 minutes for the whole trip, this was a remarkably fast service. Two photographs of this rare working are reproduced. The train gave a foretaste of how the new trains could have transformed services on the Fermanagh lines if the closures had not been pushed through so soon. The matter was debated in the Northern Ireland Senate, where the new service was praised for its speed and comfort. Senator O'Hare urged the government to grant a two year suspension of the closure and claimed that fifty people had used the service when he travelled. However the debate centred less on the potential of the new service than on the fact that, in the photograph of the train in that morning's Northern Whig, only twelve people were visible!

The express diesel just north of Portadown, at Cumo level crossing. Notice that the trailer is now facing the opposite way after changing direction at Omagh.

A Mystery

There is another intriguing aspect to the circumstances surrounding the closure. It is perhaps not fully realised that most of the passengers on the 'Bundoran Express' travelled, not to Bundoran, but to Pettigo. Pettigo was the railhead for a pilgrimage to Lough Derg, a few miles away, buses being used for the last part of the journey. An island in Lough Derg was the renowned site of St Patrick's Purgatory, and was the oldest religious site in Ireland. The pilgrims who used the 'Bundoran Express' mostly came from the Republic of Ireland, from Dublin, Drogheda, Dundalk, Clones, etc, and the train ran non-stop through Northern Ireland to avoid customs delays. This train ran during the pilgrimage season (1 June-15 August) and was very important to the people of the South.

The writer 'Barney McCool' told me that on one occasion in 1957 he was at Bundoran Junction and spoke to a signalman there. Commenting on the pending closure he said "Isn't it dreadful about the railway going to close," to which the signalman replied, "Sure it's not going to close. Lot of nonsense. If it was going to close why would they be fixing the track up? Anyway isn't the Southern Government going to pay them to keep it open so that the 'pilgrim train' can run?" (This may not be the exact conversation, but certainly the gist of it.) 'Barney' put this down to the man being misinformed but, in more recent years, he was talking to a CIE official in Dublin and mentioned this incident. To his surprise the man said "There might be something in that because in the archives at Connolly Station (the old Amiens St terminus of the GNR) there is a file of correspondence between the Southern and Northern governments over that very subject." It would be intriguing to know more about this because, if it is true, the whole story of the closures has not yet been told and it may be that the government of the Irish Republic was prepared to go to remarkable lengths to keep the GNR open, and the Northern Ireland government equally determined to close it.

The Last Day

Despite all the last minute calls for a reprieve, the Northern Ireland government pressed ahead with the closures, promising Fermanagh improvements to bus services and a new high speed road through the Clogher Valley to Belfast. The SLNCR had no alternative but to announce that its services too would terminate on 30 September 1957. Thus it was that on that one date the entire rail services of a complete county were to be eliminated, a situation that to my knowledge is unique in these islands.

For the record, the movements of the last trains in Fermanagh were as follows. On the Bundoran branch the 2.25 pm Bundoran to Enniskillen, with loco 42 and two coaches, was crewed by Davy Armstrong and Paddy Love. At Pettigo they met No 73, with two coaches and a van, on the 2.05 pm Enniskillen to Bundoran and at Irvinestown they overtook the up goods which had left Bundoran some time earlier. After arriving at Bundoran at 4.05 pm, No 73 worked the empty carriages to Omagh at 5.30 pm.

On the Enniskillen-Omagh line the last Down train was the 6.40 pm, consisting of two coaches and a van, hauled by No 74, with engine crew Arthur Darragh and Billy Hawthorne and guard Fred Cahill from Ballinamallard. Behind No 74, on this train, was No 155 (a goods engine) driven by Barney McGirr of Omagh with fireman Peter Judge. In the opposite direction came No 197 *Lough Neagh* (a blue engine) on the 5.30 pm from Derry (7.23 pm from Omagh). It was crewed by Freddy Rankin and Norman Brown and the guard was Herbert Wilson. Later in the evening, the express diesel from Belfast terminated in Omagh and the Enniskillen passengers changed into a steam train, departing at 8.45 pm and arriving in Enniskillen at 9.25 pm.

Meanwhile at Enniskillen, No 42 with two coaches had worked the 6.20 pm to Clones (normally a railcar or railbus). In the opposite direction the last train from Clones, and the last to arrive in Enniskillen from any direction, was the 9.45 pm which arrived six minutes late at 10.39 pm. The engine was 196 *Lough Gill*, crewed by Jimmy Armstrong and Victor Coulter, with Thomas Hilliard as guard .

Similar scenes were played out on the SLNCR. Here the last train out of Enniskillen was the 7.25 pm mixed hauled by 0-6-4T *Lough Melvin* driven by Gerry O'Connor and fired by Bertie Hegarty, both Sligo men. It arrived in Sligo almost an hour late at 10.30 pm. In the other direction came Patrick Nevin of Enniskillen driving Railcar B (his regular charge) on the 4.00 pm from Sligo arriving at 6.20 pm. The guard was Richard Rooney of Sligo.

After the Closures

Fermanagh's stations fell eerily quiet on the night of 30 September 1957. There was a small amount of activity in the days that followed, as station-masters supervised the packing of equipment into boxes and its dispatch by special train to Dundalk. They then turned the keys on the stations for the last time, and they became silent and ghostly. For many of the older men it was the end of their railway careers. A lot of the

young ones, sensing that future prospects were poor, left the railway at that time too. Those that stayed on were transferred to other areas, like Omagh, Portadown or Belfast. Even the days of the GNR were numbered. The Northern Ireland government pressed for the termination of the GNR Board agreement, and in the end the Irish Republic accepted the inevitable. On 1 October 1958 the official existence of the GNR ended and its movable assets were divided between CIE and the UTA. They were divided equally (each company, for

Top far left: The crew of the last train to Omagh, driver Arthur Darragh and fireman Billy Hawthorne.

Top near left: Pettigo on the last day. No 42, with driver Davy Armstrong and fireman Paddy Love has the last train to Enniskillen and has just crossed No 73 on the last train to Bundoran.

Middle left: The last goods train leaving Bundoran at 11.20 am, hauled by PG 0-6-0 No 100. It consists of a wagon, two vans and a brake van.

Bottom left: The last passenger train in the Omagh direction was the 6.40 pm, seen here about to set out from Enniskillen with Nos 74 and 155. No 155 was only the pilot, but GNR practice was for the bogie engine to lead if the pilot was an 0-6-0.

Right: Driver Paddy Nevin poses at the controls of Railcar B, which had just worked the last ever Sligo Leitrim train into Enniskillen at 6.15 pm. Railcar B was Paddy's pride and joy.

instance, getting 83 steam locomotives) because the £4.5M used to purchase the company had been borne equally.

This did not really affect the Fermanagh lines as the only UTA trains that ever ran on them were the lifting trains, but officially the lines were now part of the UTA system. After another year the UTA began lifting the lines, the first to go being the Glaslough to Portadown section of the line from Clones, which was lifted in late 1959. Early in 1960 the Clones to Enniskillen line was severed at the Northern Ireland border near Clones, and the lifting gangs gradually worked back to Enniskillen, reaching Lisnaskea in the summer and Enniskillen in the autumn. One Enniskillen schoolboy spent his holidays getting a free ride on this train and continued doing this when term resumed! It was two weeks before his parents discovered he was not at school!

The track gangs then moved on to the Enniskillen-Bundoran Junction section in the autumn and, having reached the Junction, halted there and lifted the branch itself, starting at Belleek. This left the Belleek-Bundoran stretch in situ and it was still there in 1962 as Charles comments in his recollections. The Bundoran branch lifting took until mid-1961, and the gang was still at Kesh in April. Once Bundoran Junction was reached the lifting of the Bundoran Junction-Omagh section resumed, Omagh finally being reached early in 1962.

Meanwhile the Sligo Leitrim was disappearing as well. Here too there were trains in the week following the closure, as rolling stock was concentrated at Enniskillen and Manorhamilton. The SLNCR bus routes were taken over by CIE as from 1 October 1957. In contrast to the GNR, the SLNCR was a privately owned railway and the company itself was being wound up. This was done at a meeting of shareholders in Dublin on 14 November 1957. A new company, the SLNCR Co Ltd was created on 17 December 1957 to attend to the winding-up and disposal of assets. These were sold in public auctions at Enniskillen (1 October 1958) and Manorhamilton (28-9 April 1959). The Fermanagh section of the Sligo Leitrim was lifted in late 1958, immediately after the Enniskillen auction.

All the rolling stock went for scrap with the exception of Railcar B and locomotives *Lough Melvin* and *Lough Erne*. Railcar B was purchased by CIE and travelled under its own power from Enniskillen to Dublin,

Above: A derelict Enniskillen, exactly one year after the closure, photographed by John Gillham on 1 October 1958, the first day of UTA ownership. This was also the day of the public auction of the movable assets of the SLNCR at Enniskillen, probably taking place immediately behind the photographer (see opposite).

Below: In much happier days we see the same scene with the station busy. Judging by the long excursion train at the Sligo platform, this is the last Sunday in July — Garland Sunday, a religious pilgrimage to Sligo. To the right of this is a substantial train, probably an excursion for Bundoran, whilst No 44 is getting another heavy train under way in the Clones direction.

The Sligo yard at Enniskillen on the same date. The wagons in the background, along with Railbus A, Railcar B and 0-6-4Ts *Lough Erne*, *Lough Melvin* and *Enniskillen*, were being auctioned, the latter fetching £475 scrap value. Apart from the weeds, little has changed from the similar view 26 years earlier, on page 116.

via Omagh and Portadown on 31 October 1958. On CIE it was numbered 2509 and ran until the 1970s. It still exists at Mallow, Co Cork, owned by the Great Southern Preservation Society, but in scrap condition and endangered. The two locomotives were purchased by the UTA (though from Beyer Peacock, the builders, due to the hire purchase agreement) and moved to Belfast in 1959. There they were numbered 26 and 27 respectively, retaining their names. They shunted at various locations — Great Victoria Street, Adelaide, York Road and the docks — for many years, 26 *Lough Melvin* being retired in 1965 and 27 *Lough Erne* in 1970. On retirement, *Lough Erne* was privately preserved by Roy Grayson, but is now owned by the Railway Preservation Society of Ireland. It has not run since 1971.

Could the Fermanagh railways have survived?

Today, looking back, it is interesting to speculate as to what would have happened to the railways in Fermanagh if political considerations had not forced their closure in 1957. Certainly the SLNCR could not have lasted much longer. Even if the two governments had decided to take it over or subsidise it, the live cattle trade was in decline anyway. The spread of refrigeration meant that by the late 1960s most cattle were slaughtered locally and then transported as meat. In both Ireland and Britain the movement of live cattle by rail ended in 1975. Even at that date Dublin-Holyhead was the only route still taking them.

Likewise the Bundoran branch could hardly have survived much beyond the early 1960s. Even in the 1950s it carried little passenger traffic in the winter and was dependent on summer holiday makers and Lough Derg pilgrims for revenue. However social changes were threatening this traffic also, with cheap continental holidays replacing the traditional week at the seaside. Today Bundoran would probably not attract enough day trippers to sustain a railway. Ballyshannon might have had some potential for replacing Sligo as a CIE freight railhead for south Donegal.

As to the other GNR lines, we can speculate that the healthy goods traffic from Enniskillen to Belfast and Derry would probably have declined in line with trends elsewhere. The UTA was to end all rail-borne freight in 1965, so that would have ended it in Fermanagh at that point, even if the Portadown-Derry line had remained open. If the UTA, and its successor NIR, had retained rail freight originating within Northern Ireland, it is possible that Enniskillen might still do some business in cement and timber traffic — perhaps three trains a week.

On the passenger side, the pattern elsewhere would suggest that the number of passengers travelling by rail (particularly local traffic) would have continued to fall until the early 1960s as car ownership spread. It would then have stabilised and, if the troubles in Northern Ireland had not taken place, the Fermanagh railways could well have benefited from tourism. The emphasis would have been on a fast service to Belfast, with a connection for Derry at Omagh. Intermediate stations between Clones and Enniskillen would have been better placed for survival than those between Enniskillen and Omagh, where the stations at Trillick, Dromore Road and Fintona Junction were too remote from the villages they served. Even so, all of them would probably have become unstaffed halts.

South of the border a useful move would have been for CIE to change the track layout at Cavan, where there was an end-on connection with the old MGWR route from Inny Junction. This would have allowed through running between Dublin and the GNR branch from Clones. In this event a through service from Dublin serving Cavan, Clones and Monaghan might have been viable for both passengers and freight. The old GNR route from Clones to Dundalk could have been abandoned and, if the UTA/NIR had retained the Armagh line, there could have been joint operation of the Monaghan-Armagh section. Such a route should have been as viable as the Dublin-Westport line is today, and a connection at Clones would have fed traffic into and out of Fermanagh. If all this had happened we would probably today have two coach NIR trains from Belfast running to Omagh, changing direction and going to Enniskillen, to terminate at Clones, and connect into a Dublin-Clones-Armagh-Belfast service. Manned level crossings would have given way to automatic half barriers, and one signal box in Portadown or Omagh would control the entire route to Clones!

All speculation perhaps, but we are entitled to dream!

Lough Melvin, as UTA No 26, at Adelaide shed, Belfast, on 10 June 1961, in the company of two UTA (ex-NCC) 2-6-4Ts. Despite appearances, the 1949-built Sligo tank is about the same age as the UTA tanks!

40

FERMANAGH'S RAILWAYS IN PICTURES

Charles P Friel

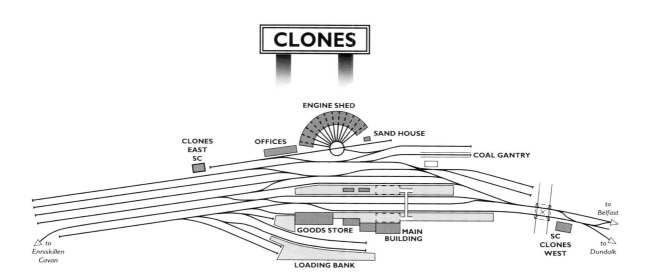

CLONES

ENGINE SHED

CLONES EAST SC

OFFICES

SAND HOUSE

COAL GANTRY

GOODS STORE

MAIN BUILDING

SC CLONES WEST

to Belfast

to Dundalk

to Enniskillen Cavan

LOADING BANK

Opposite top: We begin our pictorial coverage of Fermanagh's railways in County Monaghan, naturally enough! Clones lies very close to the south-eastern corner of Fermanagh and, before 1921, was the nearest big town for much of south Fermanagh. For the rail traveller it was often the point of access to the county and it would be highly inappropriate to omit this interesting and, occasionally, very busy junction.

Our first photo shows a train from Dundalk arriving past Clones East signal cabin and making its way into the back of the island platform. The locomotive is 1915 built U class 4-4-0 No 200 *Lough Melvin,* here in the GNR's passenger livery of lined blue. The three coaches are led by a J⁴ brake composite and, typical of the line, there is a long tail of vans at the back of the train. The first two are 20 ton capacity P vans. Their working was strictly rostered and we may guess that this is the 10.45 am from Dundalk.

Opposite bottom: Our second view of Clones is from the same vantage point as the first but now looking west through the passenger station where the Up 'Bundoran Express' is waiting to leave for Dundalk and Dublin. The main station building is on the left and the island platform on the right. Most GNR footbridges were closed-in affairs with a rounded roof of corrugated iron, but Clones' footbridge was quite open and flat roofed. This is 11 August 1957, a Sunday, so the time must be about 3.40 pm. The locomotive is one of the 1948-built U class 4-4-0s — No 204 *Antrim.*

To the extreme right is a glimpse of the roof of Clones engine shed — a partial roundhouse, built in 1924 just after Portadown's similar structure. Unlike Portadown though, Clones shed is still standing and in use. Note the six-coach rake at Platform 2.

Above: Looking east from platform 1, we see the shunting engine, AL class 0-6-0 No 140, resting between duties in the middle road below the footbridge and alongside the AEC diesel railcar set which has just worked the 7.45 am from Belfast. The distinctive spire of the Roman Catholic church is visible in this May 1956 view.

Opposite top: At the west end of platform 1 we see P6'6" class 4-4-0 No 72 with a two coach train for Cavan on 18 April 1955.

Opposite bottom: SG3 class 0-6-0 No 49 pauses in the middle road with a goods train consisting mostly of 8 ton open wagons. Fifteen of these heavy goods locomotives were built in 1920-21.

Below: Our final view of Clones is of PP class 4-4-0 No 74 storming away with a long excursion train for Bundoran on Sunday 25 July 1954. To the left of the train is the water tower and, behind it, the coaling gantry where wagons of coal, on a siding about eight feet above the running line, fed coal to the waiting engines.

NEWTOWNBUTLER

Opposite top: This is one of the oldest photographs in the book and was taken from an Enniskillen-bound train stopped at Newtownbutler in October 1897. The cameraman was no less than L J Watson, the GNR(I)'s chief locomotive draughtsman, who was in effect the designer of some of Ireland's most successful locomotives. He was a keen photographer and, although using glass negatives for locomotive portraits, had bought a roll-film camera in Dublin earlier that month. This view is from the first film he took with it. Newtownbutler station building was designed by W G Murray in the Gothic revival style, and is still inhabited. Note the enamelled advertisements for Tylers boots and Lifebuoy soap. If you look closely you can just see a wee boy being brought up to see the engine!

Opposite bottom: Another view of an Enniskillen-bound passenger train, this time dating from 18 April 1955. The locomotive is 197 *Lough Neagh,* another of the 1915 batch of U class 4-4-0s. The loop to the left could hold up to 38 wagons and a locomotive, but had no passenger platform.

Above: Newtownbutler's signal cabin was at the west end of the station with the loop just in front of it and the running line nearer the camera. The goods yard is to the right. At the platform is UG class 0-6-0 No 147 with the 4.30 pm Dundalk to Enniskillen passenger train, due here between 5.17 and 5.22 pm. The date is 8 July 1957.

Above: Sallaghy level crossing was between Newtownbutler and Lisnaskea, fairly close to the latter. On 19 May 1960 the UTA lifting train is seen crossing the Lisnaskea-Crom road at this point. The locomotive is SG2 0-6-0 No 42 (Ex GNR 183), built in 1915. By this time the line had been closed for nearly three years and weeds are very much in evidence. The neat GNR crossing keeper's house is on the left, and its occupants watch the passing train.

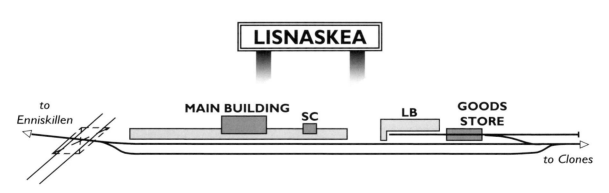

Opposite top: Lisnaskea, like Newtownbutler, had a passing loop (mainly for use by goods trains) but only one passenger platform. In this view we are looking west past the signal cabin to where U class 4-4-0 No 198 *Lough Swilly* has the 1.25 pm from Londonderry (Foyle Road) to Dundalk (arriving here at 5.36 pm, and not due in Dundalk until 7.24 pm!) The date is Easter Monday, 2 April 1956. The jet of steam below the bufferbeam is a leak from the train heating which took steam, at 40 psi, into pipes beneath the seats. The level crossing gates are visible in the distance.

Right: A group of railway men beside Lisnaskea signal cabin in 1930. From the left they are William Smith, William Symington, Oliver Ramsey, James Elliott, C Collins, the Stationmaster J Scott and his son Teddy. This view is looking towards Clones and shows the goods shed with an open wagon in the doorway. To the extreme right, beyond the Up starting signal, is the cattle loading bank — or 'beach' to railwaymen.

Above: U class 4-4-0 No 204 *Antrim* pauses at Lisnaskea with a Clones to Enniskillen passenger train in 1957. The guard and the station porter seem to be taking particular care in loading a lady's bicycle into the guards van.

MAGUIRESBRIDGE

Opposite top: Maguiresbridge looking east towards Clones. The signal cabin is to the right at the Enniskillen end of the Down platform with the white level crossing gates marking where the road crosses the line. The Down platform had a small waiting shelter but the main station building is at the Up platform in the middle of the picture. This picture dates from after the closure of the Clogher Valley Railway and shows grass where the 3ft gauge CVR tracks used to be, to the left of the main station building (see page 52). Two GNR open wagons are at the goods store to the extreme left.

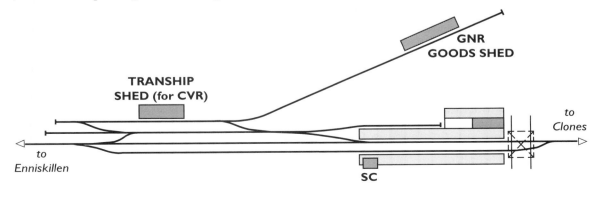

Below: This delightful view of Maguiresbridge is looking towards Enniskillen on Saturday 18 July 1953. Here P6'6" class 4-4-0 No 73 waits, on the right, while working the 1.15 pm from Clones to Enniskillen. This was usually a railbus duty. Coming the other way is PP class 4-4-0 No 12 with a Bundoran to Belfast special composed, it seems, entirely of low elliptical roofed coaches. Note the way 'Maguiresbridge' appears on the signal cabin.

Above: An unusual locomotive in these parts was Q class 4-4-0 No 133 here approaching Maguiresbridge from Enniskillen. These larger 4-4-0s did not often work in Fermanagh. The wagons in the siding to the right include an engineer's six-wheel three-plank open wagon with sleepers, coupled to a 25-ton brake van, one of a batch built in Belgium just before World War One.

The Clogher Valley Railway

MAGUIRESBRIDGE

Above: Maguiresbridge in 1939. On the right we can see the GNR siding which terminates before the platform. On the extreme right the fence obscures a view of the GNR broad gauge platform. The narrow gauge platform and lines are to the left. No 6 *Erne*, having arrived earlier from Fivemiletown, has now turned and is taking water, prior to making the return journey.

Top: Looking in the opposite direction in 1937, we get a clearer view of the narrow gauge side of the station. The main passenger building is on the left and the Clogher Valley's water tower on the right. In the distance is the transshipment shed, where goods traffic was exchanged between broad gauge GNR wagons on the left and narrow gauge CVR ones on the right. The wicker hampers on the platform may well contain fresh bread.

Centre: Maguiresbridge in 1937 showing the Clogher Valley lines

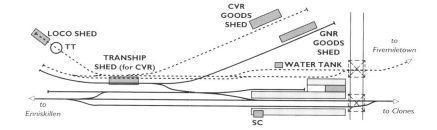

Bottom: On 14 May 1920, No 3 *Blackwater* has arrived with the 11.30 am mixed train from Fivemiletown. This is a particularly significant picture for my co-author Norman, as his grandfather William Johnston was still Station Master when it was taken, and his father and uncle were small boys living at the station. No 3 still has the original large headlamp and further down the platform, a porter is unloading luggage onto a hand trolley.

53

Below: A close up of the transship shed in 1937. The 5'3" gauge lines of the GNR are to the left and the 3'0" gauge Clogher Valley lines to the right. As you can see, there wasn't much shelter and, the growth of weeds suggests, not much use either! The CVR's seldom photographed engine shed is visible in the right background.

Opposite top: A train for Fivemiletown is seen at Maguiresbridge in 1933. The locomotive is No 6 *Erne*, one of six identical 0-4-2T locomotives built for the opening of the line in 1887. Because of the roadside tramway nature of much of the CVR track, the locomotives had sheet metal cow-catchers and side skirts to hide the wheels and motion. For safety reasons, the locomotives ran cab first and had a large acetylene lamp to help at night. The water was carried in side tanks and the coal in a bunker placed across the top of the firebox. The leading vehicle in the train is third class bogie No 15, which accommodated 40 passengers on longitudinally placed seats that were originally bare wood, but which had been upholstered about 1930. The coach has verandah ends. Behind the coach is brake van No 2, one of six such vehicles. It too has a verandah at one end and a large sliding door on each side to accommodate the mails and parcels traffic. At the rear of the train is one of the line's thirty cattle wagons. They, like the coach and the locomotive, were built for the opening in 1887.

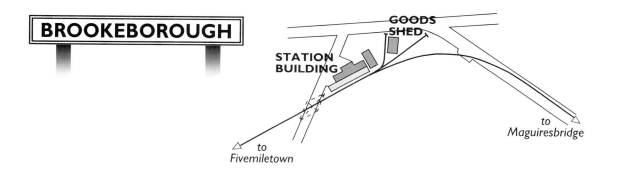

Below: Brookeborough, the first station out of Maguiresbridge, had a substantial passenger building and two goods sidings but no loop. Here we are looking east, towards Fivemiletown, on 29 June 1937. The Station Master (or agent) lived in the two-storey part of the building, where the station nameboard was mounted. The level crossing gates, at the far end of the station, were a fairly recent, and lightweight, replacement for the originals, which were demolished one Sunday morning when diesel rail tractor No 2 ran away. The driver, Joe Murphy, escaped injury by retreating into the train well before impact! 'The Unit' carried a permanent reminder of the crash when the damage was repaired by cutting away its lower cab-sheets (see page 27).

Above: Stonepark halt was situated at a crossroads on the Fivemiletown side of Brookeborough, quite close to Colebrooke station. In this view, No 6 *Erne* is heading towards Maguiresbridge on 25 June 1937. The guard is probably studying the photographer, Henry Casserley, to ascertain whether or not he wants the train to stop.

Below: Colebrooke station as it is today. The line ran beyond the building. This station was built to serve the Colebrooke Estate, owned by the Brooke family to this day. Sir Basil Brooke, later Lord Brookeborough, was Prime Minister of Northern Ireland from 1943 to 1963. The station ceased to feature in CVR timetables in the 1930s and became an unstaffed halt.

Right: A builder's photograph of No 5 *Colebrooke* showing the locomotive in its original condition, with condenser. We can see that the cow-catcher was fitted at one end only. The huge original oil lamp can be seen on the backplate, its chimney rising above the line of the cab. Below the side tanks are four hinged and two sliding inspection doors. Comparing with the picture of No 6 (opposite) we can see some changes. The original doors were too light and rattled a lot. They

were replaced with a heavier gauge of metal and more substantial hinges. The ones below the cab door and alongside the cylinders were dispensed with. Looking higher up, we can see that there is as yet no coal bunker. The whistle is mounted on the cab roof, and the Ramsbottom safely valves on top of the dome, which is placed quite far back. Alongside the chimney can be seen the condensing pipes which fed the exhaust steam into the side tanks. The condensing steam caused problems with the engines' injectors which preferred cold water. Note too, the bell, mounted on top of the boiler and the large maker's plate on the smokebox — Sharp Stewart & Co, Limited, Atlas Works, 3373 - 1887 Manchester. 3373 was the maker's number. The photo has been embossed by the North British Locomotive Company who took over Sharp Stewart in 1903.

Above: Corralongford halt was in Fermanagh and was located two miles west of Fivemiletown. Like other CVR halts, its facilities were minimal, consisting of a bench seat, a nameboard and a noticeboard for timetables and posters. This view shows well the CVR trackbed, usually running on the verge to one side of the road.

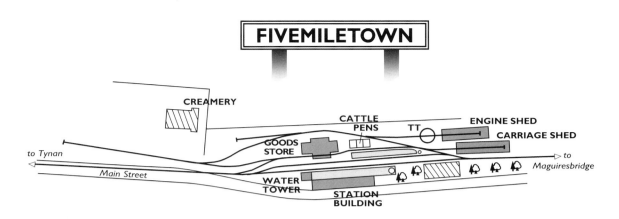

FIVEMILETOWN

CREAMERY

CATTLE PENS   TT   ENGINE SHED   CARRIAGE SHED

GOODS STORE

to Tynan

Main Street

WATER TOWER

STATION BUILDING

to Maguiresbridge

Opposite top: Another Tynan-bound train at Fivemiletown is here in the charge of No 6 and may well be the same train that we saw earlier at Maguiresbridge.

Here the coach, brake van and cattle wagon have been joined by two further cattle wagons. One of the cattle wagons is higher than the others — it was one of six that could be used for conveying horses. All the other cattle wagons could be converted to carry goods traffic by closing the ventilators below the roof.

Below: Fivemiletown station with an as yet engine-less train for Tynan at the platform. In keeping with CVR architecture, Fivemiletown's Station Master had two storey accommodation. The ticket office was behind the glazed wooden screen, though its clock is absent. The water tower is just visible on the right, while, to the left, is the goods store with a van alongside.

Below: We finish our coverage of Fivemiletown with a look in the Maguiresbridge direction, sometime in 1933. The building to the left is the engine shed with its turntable. Alongside is a carriage shed. Notice that its wall, next the running line, is not carried down to the ground. This was to provide ventilation and to help vehicles dry out in wet weather. Note the water column, with its leather bag blowing in the wind, and the high operating handle, so that the firemen could control the watering operation while standing on top of the locomotive's tanks.

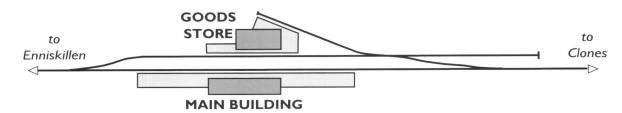

LISBELLAW

to Enniskillen

GOODS STORE

MAIN BUILDING

to Clones

Opposite top: We return to the Great Northern to continue our progress towards Enniskillen. Lisbellaw was another one-platform station with a loop alongside. On Saturday 7 April 1956 No 198 *Lough Swilly* sweeps in with the 10.45 am passenger train from Dundalk to Omagh, while those waiting to board the train get ready to look for seats. Behind the three coaches is another string of vans for all the parcels traffic, mails and perishable sundries. To the left we see the first of several station names set out in six foot tall concrete letters. They were also to be seen at Lisnaskea, Enniskillen, Trillick and Dromore Road stations.

Opposite bottom: Going the other way is PP class 4-4-0 No 106 with the 4 pm Enniskillen to Clones passenger train on Easter Monday, 2 April 1956. The splendid four-coach train would normally be a 'mixed' — ie with goods wagons on the tail and a brake van at the end. Maybe during a holiday there was no goods traffic.

Above: Lisbellaw's main station building is seen from a coach on the same train as in the previous picture, the 4 pm from Enniskillen, but 18 months later, on Saturday 7 September 1957.

Above: A delightful study of PP class 4-4-0 No 42 departing with the 7.40 pm to Bundoran at the west end of Enniskillen on 20 July 1954.

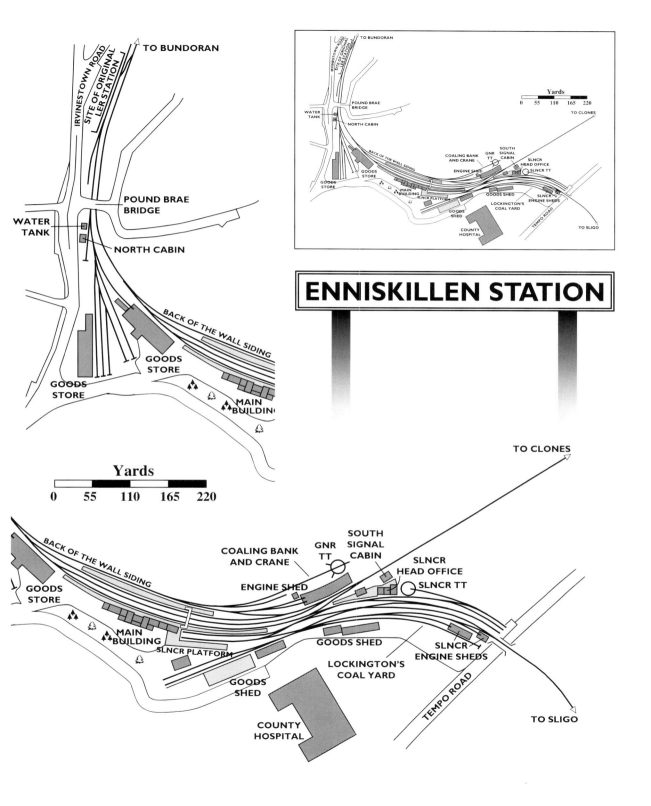

TO BUNDORAN

IRVINESTOWN ROAD

SITE OF ORIGINAL LER STATION

POUND BRAE BRIDGE

WATER TANK

NORTH CABIN

BACK OF THE WALL SIDING

GOODS STORE

GOODS STORE

MAIN BUILDING

ENNISKILLEN STATION

Yards

0   55   110   165   220

TO CLONES

BACK OF THE WALL SIDING

COALING BANK AND CRANE

GNR TT

SOUTH SIGNAL CABIN

SLNCR HEAD OFFICE

SLNCR TT

ENGINE SHED

GOODS STORE

MAIN BUILDING

SLNCR PLATFORM

GOODS SHED

GOODS SHED

LOCKINGTON'S COAL YARD

SLNCR ENGINE SHEDS

TEMPO ROAD

COUNTY HOSPITAL

TO SLIGO

Opposite top: On the Lisbellaw side of Enniskillen, No 204 *Antrim* is working the Up 'Bundoran Express' on 10 July 1957 and is seen here alongside the Tempo Road, just visible on the left. To the right is the Killynure siding, empty on this occasion. The express is made up of just five carriages; often it was longer. The through coach for Belfast is at the back of the train.

Opposite bottom: Enniskillen South. SG3 class 0-6-0 No 40 shows a 'slow goods train' lampcode on the front bufferbeam as it rolls though the deep cutting past the South signal cabin with the goods from Clones due here at 10 am. Enniskillen's locomotive shed is to the left and the Sligo Leitrim's headquarters to the right. In the foreground is the only track connecting the GNR and SLNCR. This 1921-built locomotive was numbered 201 up to April 1948, when that number went to one of the new U class 4-4-0s.

Above: It is just after 1.30 pm on 20 May 1954 as U class 4-4-0 No 196 *Lough Gill* rolls past Enniskillen shed with the 10.45 am from Dundalk. To the right of the South cabin, one of the two newest Sligo Leitrim 0-6-4Ts is sitting alongside the company offices. An SLNCR brakevan is just visible on the extreme right.

Opposite top: Railcar C₃ with trailer No 847 leaves Enniskillen with the 6.20 pm service to Clones on 26 May 1953. On the left is part of the Sligo Leitrim goods yard. In the centre of the picture, beyond the railcar trailer, stands one of the GNR clerestory-roofed six-wheel passenger vans. The lines at the bottom right of the picture lead to the engine shed — the left hand one has a pit which allowed enginemen access to the motion of a locomotive and this is where engine ashpans were cleaned.

Opposite bottom: This scene is looking into Enniskillen station from the Clones end of No 1 platform in May 1950. The short canopy on the extreme left marks where the Sligo Leitrim had its passenger platform. Below the footbridge PP class 4-4-0 No 46 waits to leave with a train for Clones. To the right the fireman is sitting down as AL class 0-6-0 No 32 propels cattle wagons into the 'back of the wall' siding. Those who know Enniskillen can get their bearings from Cole's monument, just at the right of the Up starting signal.

Above: The time should be 11.37 am because this picture shows, on the right, the arrival of the AEC diesel train from Belfast via Clones. Power car 603 is leading and 602 was at the other end. The train on the left, at platform 1, is the stock for the 12 noon to Omagh — its engine has yet to come from the shed. The wagon nearest the camera has a bread container.

Opposite top: Enniskillen shed on 11 August 1951, with at least three locomotives 'on shed'. To the left is a very clean SG3 class 0-6-0 No 117, probably for that evening's goods to Derry at 9.40 pm. The engine to the right is PP class 4-4-0 No 44. The tender between them belongs to LQG 0-6-0 No 160. To the extreme left is the grounded six-wheel coach body that was used as sleeping quarters by some engine crews. Beyond that is the crane used for coaling engines. The turntable is hidden behind 117's right hand lamp bracket. The wagons on the right are being shunted to the SLNCR yard.

Opposite bottom: A closer view of Enniskillen shed in late September 1957 and a lovely portrait of P6'6" class 4-4-0 No 73. Modellers will want to note how the shed curved to follow the Clones line on the right. The cutting beyond the back of shed survives today as a footpath.

Above: Railbus 4 is seen here working the 6.20 pm to Clones on 20 July 1954. This railbus dates from 1935 and was built at Dundalk for service on the Dundalk, Newry and Greenore Railway. It was sold back to the GNR in 1947. Just visible at the back of the bus are the steps used to enter and leave the vehicle at level crossings.

Opposite top: The Down 'Bundoran Express' eases through Enniskillen in August 1957 hauled by No 204. On the left is the diesel train from Belfast which had arrived at 11.37 am. This is about 12.27 pm. The diesel was booked to depart to Belfast at 12.30 pm after the 'Express' had cleared the Lisbellaw-Enniskillen section.

Opposite bottom: In this 1955 view, looking north west from platform 1, a train from Omagh is sitting at platform 2 and AL 0-6-0 No 59 is sitting in the middle road with bread containers. Clearly visible next the engine is a Brewster container and, on the same wagon, a Stevenson container is partially visible.

Above: Photographs of the exterior of Enniskillen seem to be quite rare — maybe the photographers were all too busy inside! This view is taken from the path up from Westville, with the goods yard and the Pound Brae away to the left. The portion of wall between the two cars is the only bit still in existence. The large board beside the door under the awning gives a list of arrival and departure times.

Opposite top: A busy scene at the west end of Enniskillen station, sometime in 1955, as 4-4-0 No 204 *Antrim* (on the left) arrives with the 10.50 am from Omagh. To the right, older sister, No 199 *Lough Derg*, waits for the road at the end of the 'back of the wall' siding, so called because it ran behind the wall of the Up platform. The name 'Enniskillen' is proclaimed in six foot high letters on the bank beyond 199's smokebox.

Opposite bottom: Railcar C$_2$ at Enniskillen in 1939. Three of these single cab, articulated cars were built at Dundalk in 1934-5, numbered C^1 (originally C), C$_2$ and C$_3$. As C^1 had to be turned at the end of each journey, the last two were intended to run back to back to avoid the need for turning on Dublin suburban duties. One car would tow and the trailing car was left in neutral gear. After World War Two, they more commonly ran as single units, as C$_2$ is doing here. One of these cars was a regular on the Bundoran branch, particularly in the winter, and the rails on the turntable at Bundoran were extended to accommodate it.

Above: The 2.10 pm combined train for Bundoran and Omagh leaves Enniskillen in late September 1957. From pictures taken that day we can surmise that the locomotives are PP class No 44 piloting P class No 73. The train is in the cutting alongside the goods shed and is traversing the most sharply curved running line on the GNR. The track was laid a half an inch wider — at 5'3½" — to allow trains an easier passage and this was safe enough at such slow speeds as the 5 mph allowed here. Enniskillen North signal cabin is partially hidden by the bank beyond the concrete name.

Opposite top: A familiar sight to many Enniskillen railwaymen was AL class 0-6-0 No 59, for long the regular shunting engine here. Delivered on New Year's Day 1894, the engine was rebuilt as shown in April 1915. She is seen here sitting near the Pound Brae bridge on an unknown date in 1956. The original Londonderry and Enniskillen Railway station was just beyond the bridge, where the wagons visible through it are sitting.

Opposite bottom: PP class 4-4-0 No 106 blowing off from both safety valves as it impatiently shunts passenger vehicles past the goods store near Enniskillen North signal cabin. This was taken from almost the same vantage point as the photograph above, but looking in the opposite direction.

Above: Heading away from Enniskillen is PP class 4-4-0 No 44 working a train for Omagh on 23 May 1955. Note the leading vehicle, a W¹ six-wheel clerestory brake. At this point the line ran parallel to the Irvinestown Road, visible in the background. Alongside No 44 is a long rake of cattle wagons, perhaps awaiting cattle for export. The hall in the right background is a gospel hall.

Opposite top: Leaving Enniskillen in the Omagh direction is this double-headed goods train. The leading locomotive is Q class 4-4-0 No 130 and the train engine appears to be a PP. The location is Drumclay, a short distance out of Enniskillen.

Opposite bottom:. In the opposite direction at the same location we see PP class 4-4-0 No 106 with the 1.25 pm Derry to Dundalk train. This train waited at Omagh from 3.02 pm until 4.17 pm! It was due in Enniskillen at 5.08 pm and Dundalk at 7.42 pm. The four passenger carriages are followed by a motley collection including two four-wheel passenger vans, a piped van and two cattle wagons. Curiously, the locomotive has only one headlamp and it is over the engine's left buffer rather than at the chimney.

GORTALOUGHAN HALT

Above:. Gortaloughan halt was 2½ miles west of Enniskillen but no trains were booked to stop there regularly. However, four Omagh-Enniskillen passenger trains and five in the other direction were timetabled to stop, if required, on weekdays. Gortaloughan had no goods facilities, so this train certainly wasn't stopping. This is the 11.20 am goods from Bundoran to Enniskillen which was due to pass here about 6 pm. The locomotive is No 73, photographed in August 1957.

BALLINAMALLARD

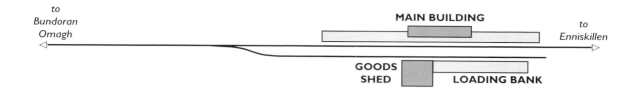

to
Bundoran
Omagh

MAIN BUILDING

to
Enniskillen

GOODS
SHED

LOADING BANK

Opposite top: Ballinamallard was another station with just one passenger platform though, despite having a goods siding, it had no loop. Here 4-4-0 No 73 arrives with a train from Bundoran to Enniskillen on 3 July 1956. There are two enthusiasts on the platform, the further one being the photographer Drew Donaldson, who took some of the photographs in this book.

Opposite bottom: UG class 0-6-0 No 79 pauses at Ballinamallard while working a Sunday excursion from Cavan to Bundoran on 8 September 1957. The signal post on the left, also visible in the previous picture, was bi-directional. Ballinamallard had no cabin and both arms seemed to be normally in the off position, except perhaps when the siding was being shunted. Presumably they were controlled by a ground frame. The trap point, preventing anything from the siding getting on to the main line, is clearly visible on the right foreground.

Above: PP class 4-4-0 No 106 is seen restarting the 12 noon Enniskillen-Omagh train away from Ballinamallard. The train comprises a six-wheel clerestory brake, a third (originally 2nd/3rd), a brake compo, a corridor compo, three cattle wagons and a bread container. This latter is probably empty and en route to either Brewster's in Derry or one of the many Belfast bakeries.

79

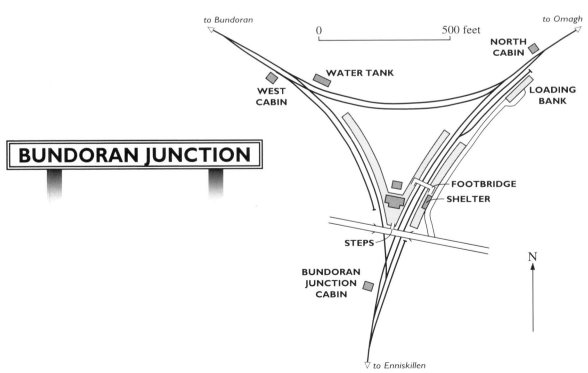

BUNDORAN JUNCTION

to Bundoran

to Omagh

0   500 feet

NORTH CABIN

WATER TANK

WEST CABIN

LOADING BANK

FOOTBRIDGE

SHELTER

STEPS

BUNDORAN JUNCTION CABIN

N

to Enniskillen

Opposite: Bundoran Junction on 8 June 1957. This is the view from the Kilskeery Road bridge and behind the nameboard are the steps leading down to the platform. Prominent is the very pleasant, glazed, Refreshment Room, built on to the front of the Station Master's house about 1910. The train visible is the 10.30 am ex Bundoran, with a passenger van at this end, waiting to continue as the 12.44 to Enniskillen. Note the water tank in the distance. A motorised luggage trolley was used to convey luggage between the Bundoran platform and the Omagh one in the foreground.

Below: Passing Bundoran Junction signal box is PP class 4-4-0 No 50 with the 12 noon from Enniskillen to Omagh on 2 June 1954. The train has the usual empty bread container at the back of the train — probably collected at Ballinamallard.

Above: From just south of the overbridge we see U class 4-4-0 No 201 *Meath* diverge on to the branch with the Down 'Bundoran Express' on 8 June 1957. Despite the almost inevitable closure of the line a mere sixteen weeks later, we can see a newly-laid turnout below the locomotive and incompletely ballasted track on both the lines to Omagh and Bundoran. An Engineer's tool van (No 8168, converted from a passenger van) is in the siding on the extreme left. Notice the sleepers and chairs scattered about on the same siding.

Below: A busy time at Bundoran Junction, as seen from the footbridge. On the left is the 1.45 pm Omagh to Enniskillen, due away from here at 2.20 pm. In the foreground is the last coach of the 2.05 pm Enniskillen to Omagh which will leave at 2.36 pm and is headed by P class No 73 (out of view). Visible through the bridge is the 2.35 pm for Bundoran with PP class 4-4-0 No 44. This engine had probably piloted the 2.05 pm which ran as a combined train from Enniskillen to Bundoran Junction. This train stopped short of the turnout for the Bundoran branch, whereupon No 44 would have run up the branch to allow No 73 to work the Omagh section forward to its platform. Then 44 would have reversed back off the branch to collect the Bundoran coaches and vans and bring them to the branch platform.The train behind 44 has seven empty cattle wagons on the tail — these might be empties being worked for a fair next day along the branch. On the other hand, if they were Omagh-bound, the locomotive on the Omagh to Enniskillen train was conveniently placed to do the honours. Busy times indeed! The signals visible here present a contrast. The signal on the left is on a white painted post of planed timber but the one beside the stone steps is a telegraph pole type made of creosoted timber. The bridge number — 178 — is visible just to the left of the Enniskillen-bound locomotive. Each bridge was given a unique number, in this case numbered from '1' at Dundalk. The Bundoran branch had its own series, beginning with '1' at Bundoran Junction.

Opposite bottom: Bundoran Junction on 2 June 1954, a view looking north from the Enniskillen side of the overbridge. Through the left-hand arch of the bridge, we see the 10.30 am from Bundoran in charge of PP class 4-4-0 No 42. You should be just able to see that, in addition to the usual passenger van, the train includes two shorter vans next the engine. This train was due here at 12.03 and will work to Enniskillen at 12.44, arriving there at 1 pm. Through the right-hand arch we see the tail of the 12 noon Enniskillen to Omagh train. To the right is the siding where the tool van was sitting in the previous photograph.

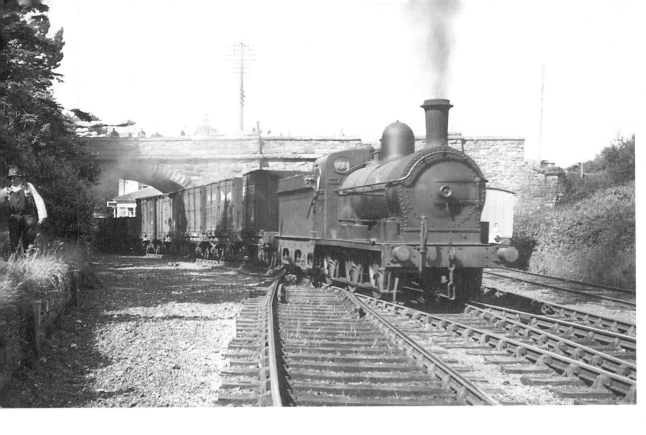

Opposite top: The Bundoran goods passes the Junction on 20 July 1956 hauled by PG class 0-6-0 No 11. This goods had left Bundoran at 11.20 am and, after serving Ballyshannon, waited at Belleek for both Bundoran Expresses to pass. Getting away from Belleek at 1.40 pm, it then got to Pettigo where it had to wait to cross the 2.35 pm from the Junction. It then served both these and Irvinestown before running non-stop to Enniskillen. It was due to pass Bundoran Junction at 4.35 pm and arrive in Enniskillen at 4.55 pm.

Opposite bottom: The Up 'Bundoran Express' passing Bundoran Junction hauled appropriately by U class 4-4-0 No 199 *Lough Derg*. To the left, the Junction signalman adapts a text-book stance as he prepares to receive the Irvinestown-Bundoran Junction staff in his left hand while holding up the Bundoran Junction to Enniskillen North staff in his right hand. The through Bundoran to Belfast coach is the fourth vehicle on the train.

Above. At the Enniskillen to Omagh platform on 2 June 1954 we see PP class 4-4-0 No 50 blowing off while working the 12 noon from Enniskillen to Omagh. On the extreme right, at the back of the platform, is milepost 70, the distance measured from zero at Dundalk.

Above: The Bundoran line platform, also on 2 June 1954. Here we see No 42 arriving with the 10.30 am from Bundoran. It will continue as the 12.44 pm to Enniskillen. In months other than June, July and August, this train would leave the Junction at 12.30 pm. In the siding on the left are at least seventeen wagons of what looks like used ballast.

Below: PP class 4-4-0 No 44 waits to leave Bundoran Junction on 12 September 1957. The train is the Bundoran portion of the 2.05 pm from Enniskillen to Omagh seen several times already. This was a continuation of the 10.45 am ex Dundalk and the first northbound train of the day scheduled to stop at Gortaloughan, if requested.

Above: Bundoran Junction West signal box was at the Bundoran end of the triangular layout. On 2 June 1954 we see No 42 arriving with the 10.30 am from Bundoran, seen with a varied collection of vacuum-fitted vehicles next the locomotive — a cattle wagon, a van, a Y class four-wheel passenger van with sliding doors and an older W class six-wheel van with double doors.

Below: Just beyond Bundoran Junction West cabin, we see PP class 4-4-0 No 74 with the two-coach 11.10 am Enniskillen to Pettigo on 2 June 1954. This train provided a service for pilgrims to Lough Derg from all stations between Enniskillen and Pettigo, arriving there at 12.22 pm. It ran from 1 June until 15 August, when Saint Patrick's Purgatory at Lough Derg closed its doors. The locomotive is running tender first as there was no turntable at Pettigo and there was no path available to run back the 15 miles to the Junction to turn.

Above: This is Tague's level crossing with No 42 on the 10.30 am from Bundoran on a wet 28 September 1957, the Saturday before the line closed. This crossing was a stopping place for several trains, as required, but latterly the only one shown in the timetables was the first train towards Bundoran, the 9.13 am (later 9.30 am) from the Junction.

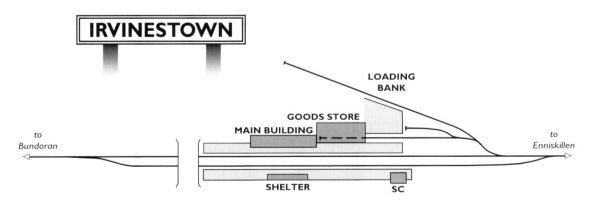

Opposite bottom: Under the road bridge at Irvinestown comes PP class 4-4-0 No 46, working the goods from Bundoran, due here at 2.15 pm, but running late in this May 1956 photograph. Marshalled just behind the locomotive are three of the distinctive bread containers which are now empty and being returned to Belfast or Londonderry. Just visible on the right is the smokebox of the locomotive (74) working the 2.35 pm passenger from the Junction to Bundoran.

Above: This view, from a Bundoran-bound train rolling into Irvinestown on 30 August 1957, gives a fine impression of this well-kept station. We can see the metal bridge carrying the road from Enniskillen across the line, towards the town, away to our right. The main station buildings are on the up platform on the right — you can see that the large door of the goods store is open. Nearer the camera is a bread wagon with two containers, for McCombs and Hughes bakeries in Belfast. Each of these containers, I was once told, could hold 28 dozen loaves!

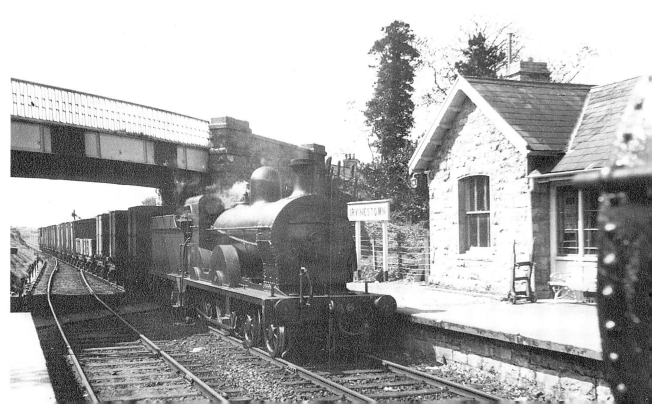

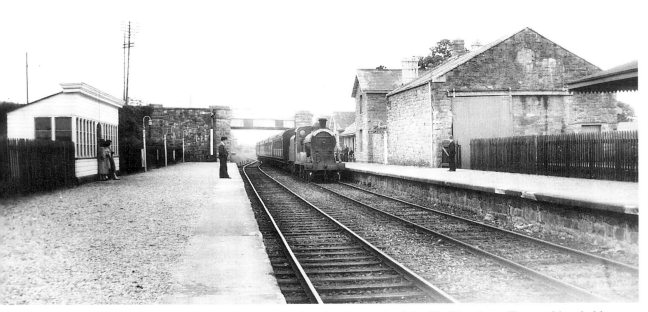

Above: In this view of Irvinestown we are observing the approach of the Up 'Bundoran Express' headed by No 201 *Meath*. On the left is the Down platform with the typical GNR shelter. On the Up platform the door of the goods shed is closed, in contrast to the previous page.

KESH

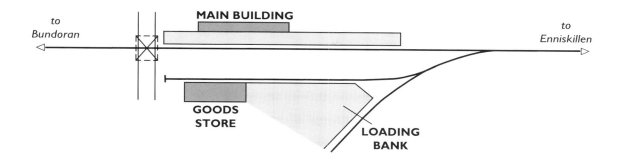

to Bundoran   MAIN BUILDING   *to Enniskillen*

GOODS STORE   LOADING BANK

Above: Kesh was the only station on the branch without a loop, but it was still a block post, as we'll see in the next photograph. The pointwork was controlled by a ground frame at the Enniskillen end of the station; another controlled the level crossing. Kesh had just two sidings and both are visible here on the left. Here No 199 has the 5.25 pm Bundoran to Enniskillen working on 21 June 1952. A permanent way bogie sits near the running line beside 199's tender.

Opposite top: Kesh at 12.55 pm on 1 September 1956, with the Down 'Bundoran Express' coming through — non-stop, of course. The signalman on the platform is holding up the staff for the Kesh to Pettigo section and will receive an Irvinestown to Kesh staff from the fireman of No 204. The scene is being watched by a couple of small boys on a station seat and by what looks like a customs man eager to pounce should the train stop or some form of contraband be thrown from it. Next the engine is a J^{11} tri-compo brake, followed by an F^{16} composite — both modern coaches at the time. In the goods sidings we see a Brewsters (of Derry) bread container and one for Inglis (of Belfast). Inglis containers were maroon but Brewsters were green with straw lettering.

Opposite bottom: Kesh, this time on a wet day. The village is to our right and the level crossing carries the road to Derry and Omagh (the route of the Omagh to Bundoran bus after 1957). Here PP class 4-4-0 No 74 has the Bundoran portion of the 2.10 pm ex Enniskillen on 4 April 1956.

Above: This is an old commercial postcard of Pettigo, taken looking east from the Bundoran end. It was one of a series published for Guest & Neville, Merchants, of Pettigo by the Doo-Well Publishing Co, Ballymena. Curiously, it was printed in Saxony (Germany). Like Irvinestown and Ballyshannon, Pettigo's goods store was part of the station buildings on the up side. Near the store are a couple of permanent way bogies and sleepers, some of them large, suggesting a resleepering of a turnout. The station has yet to acquire its footbridge, the extension to the Up platform, or the protective awnings on the Up platform seen in the following pictures.

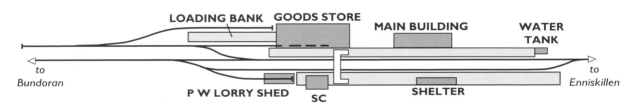

LOADING BANK   GOODS STORE

MAIN BUILDING   WATER TANK

to Bundoran

P W LORRY SHED   SC   SHELTER

to Enniskillen

Opposite top: The Up (Bundoran to Dublin) 'Bundoran Express', hauled by No 204 *Antrim*, arrives at Pettigo to stop alongside its Dublin to Bundoran counterpart. The far platform is very busy with those who have made the pilgrimage, or 'done the island' in the vernacular, and two porters are keeping passengers back from the platform edge. The protective awning of corrugated asbestos metal was erected just after the last war and gave some shelter to the pilgrims, who by this time were on their third day of fasting with virtually no sleep. In 1952 a record of almost 22,000 pilgrims used this busy station.

Opposite bottom: Pettigo was a very busy spot on any weekday in the summer between about 1.04 and 1.23 pm. This is the view from the footbridge on 18 June 1953, looking towards Bundoran. Just departed is the Down Express — a five-carriage train hauled by 199 *Lough Derg*. The carriages at the platform form the Up Express hauled by 202 *Louth*. The coach nearest the camera is a modern F^{16} corridor composite and it is followed by a clerestory-roofed M^1 bogie van. The rear coach is a brake compo, the through coach for Belfast (via Clones of course). Waiting patiently in the background is the stock of the 11.10 am from Enniskillen headed by a third U class locomotive, this time No 198 *Lough Swilly*. It will return as the 1.35 pm to Enniskillen.

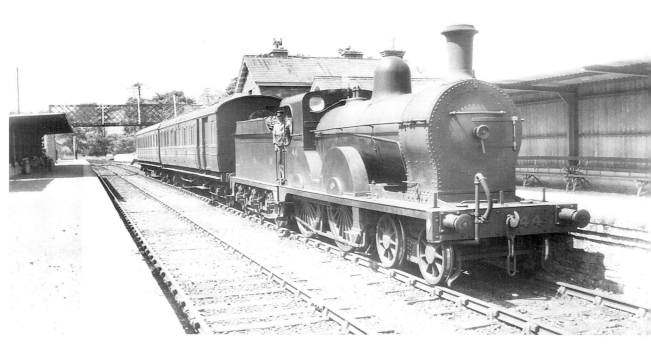

Above: After the departure of the other trains, the 1.35 pm passenger for Enniskillen would move up to the platform. On 22 June 1957 the locomotive is PP class 4-4-0 No 44. Standing proudly in the cab is driver Douglas Armstrong of Enniskillen. The first coach is a J^4 brake composite. Pilgrims from south Fermanagh stations could use the 7.50 am ex Clones to join the 11.10 am Enniskillen to Pettigo. On the homeward leg they could use the 1.35 pm as far as Enniskillen, arriving at 2.46 pm, and then wait for the 4 pm 'mixed' thence. They must have been hardy souls! Two nursing colleagues of my mother, who were going to Lough Derg, once used the 11.10 service, but they got into such a deep conversation that they lost all contact with the real world and only realised what was happening when they saw Kesh for the second time that day! Somehow the shunt at Pettigo, and the layover in the siding from 12.12 pm until 1.35 pm, totally escaped their notice!

Below: This is Ross Harbour again, but fairly soon after 26 September 1956 — the clothes suggest a Sunday, the 30 September perhaps. On 26 September part of the embankment along the edge of Lower Lough Erne gave way under a weight of flood water. A bus service replaced the trains between Pettigo and Bundoran between 27 September and the reopening of the line on 18 October 1956. The line-up of cars and motorcycles is impressive for its time.

Opposite top: The location is Ross Harbour about a mile east of Castlecaldwell, with the picturesque Lower Lough Erne alongside. Nowadays the road occupies the trackbed and the old road is a very pleasant lay-by. At the further end of the leading coach is a board reminding drivers to reduce speed at the permanent 30 mph slack between mileposts 20½ and 21¾. Castlecaldwell was at milepost 22¾, measured from the Junction. Here, on 8 September 1957, we see U class 4-4-0 No 197 *Lough Neagh* at the head of the regular Sunday excursion from Derry to Bundoran. Leaving Derry (Foyle Road) at 12.50 pm, the five coach train served Strabane, Sion Mills, Victoria Bridge, Newtownstewart and Omagh. After stopping at Fintona Junction, Dromore Road and Trillick, the train then took the direct curve at Bundoran Junction. It stopped at every station on the line, except Castlecaldwell and Belleek, before arriving in Bundoran at 3.52 pm. The return working was at 8.33 pm, though, wisely, it was advertised as departing 10 minutes earlier. Eventual arrival in Derry was at 11.46 pm. According to one of my father's sisters, who often used this train, the time in Bundoran was spent in open-air dancing near the Roguey Rocks.

Above: Castlecaldwell as seen from a Bundoran-bound train on 30 August 1957. Like Kesh, this station did not have a signal cabin, even though it was a block post. However, unlike Kesh, Castlecaldwell had a loop. Like those at some stations east of Enniskillen, the loop was normally used only for goods traffic and had its own platform. The loop was fairly short and could only hold a 20-wagon train.

GOODS STORE

to
Bundoran

to
Enniskillen

WAITING ROOM

Opposite top: Unusually here is a passenger train using the goods loop at Castlecaldwell. P6'6" class 4-4-0 No 73 is working the 10.30 am from Bundoran on 1 August 1955. The reason for this rare occurrence has not been recorded. Before the Second World War, the loop was sometimes used by empty trains waiting to pick up parties of pilgrims at Pettigo. Near the station nameboard, to the left, can be seen two sets of wooden steps which were used to cross fences at some level crossings. They were probably made at Dundalk and deposited here by the Down goods around 9 am. Judging by the passenger train, the time in this photograph is about 11.10 am.

Opposite bottom: Looking from the Bundoran end of the main platform, we see U class 4-4-0 No 205 *Down* working the 12.10 pm Sundays Only from Enniskillen to Bundoran on 8 September 1957. Leaning from the cab, holding the staff, is driver Paddy Martin. The guard is too far away to be identified but the other man on the platform is permanent way man Bob Watson, carrying a track hammer.

Above: This is Belleek, as seen from the bridge carrying the main street across the line. The train is the Down 'Bundoran Express' on 5 August 1957, hauled by U class 4-4-0 No 201 *Meath*. The train is of six bogies, the first four of which are modern — a J[11], an F[16] and two K[15] thirds. On the left a single van occupies Belleek's goods loop — the shortest on the line and capable of holding just fifteen wagons and a locomotive. Belleek's signal cabin was unusually sited — set back from the running lines rather than at the end of the platform (something like Arley on the Severn Valley Railway). The siding to the Belleek Pottery factory passed behind the cabin and ran for about 160 yards down a steep gradient before reaching the Pottery gates. The siding brought in coal, clay and other new materials, while the outward traffic was, of course, the Pottery's famous porcelain.

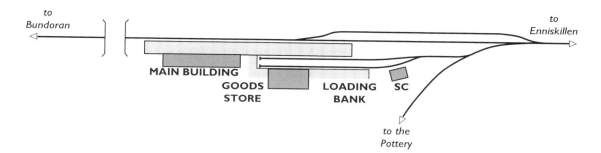

to Bundoran

to Enniskillen

MAIN BUILDING

GOODS STORE

LOADING BANK

SC

to the Pottery

Opposite top: In this view we have a clearer view of the goods store and loading bank behind the passenger platform. In the foreground is the turnout for the loop. This train, hauled by No 50, is probably the 10.30am from Bundoran. Note the loco crew relaxing on the platform.

Opposite bottom: Going the same way at Belleek is this 'Hills of Donegal' excursion on 30 May 1953. Starting at Belfast, the train ran first to Strabane, where the passengers changed to a County Donegal narrow gauge train for the journey to Ballyshannon, via Stranorlar and Donegal town. After walking though Ballyshannon to the GNR station, the passengers found their train waiting to take them on to the heady delights of Bundoran. This is the return train en route to Belfast, via Omagh, hauled by UG class 0-6-0 No 80, built in 1937. The left hand figure is driver Barney McGirr.

Above:. This is the viaduct over the Erne, just west of Belleek, on 22 June 1957, when PP class 4-4-0 No 42 was working the 10.30 am from Bundoran to the Junction, typically with two passenger vans coupled next to the locomotive. The photographer is on the County Fermanagh bank of the Erne, but the train is in County Donegal.

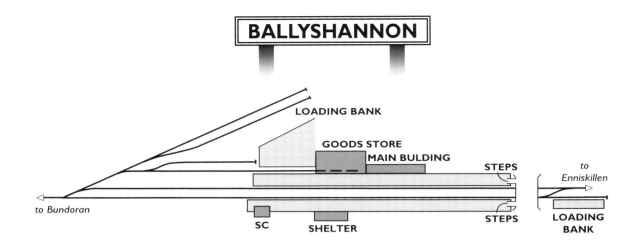

BALLYSHANNON

LOADING BANK

GOODS STORE

MAIN BULDING

STEPS

to Enniskillen

to Bundoran

SC

SHELTER

STEPS

LOADING BANK

Opposite top: We move now beyond the boundaries of County Fermanagh to complete our coverage of the Bundoran branch. Ballyshannon's Down platform on 2 August 1956 sees 4-4-0 No 74 and the 2.10 pm ex Enniskillen. The overbridge, from which the picture below was taken, is visible in the background. Below it the huddle of figures includes a white-capped Customs man and a gaggle of passengers having their luggage examined at the rear van.

Below: This is the approach to Ballyshannon from the east looking down from the road overbridge. Here we see PP class 4-4-0 No 107 approaching with the 2.40 pm from Bundoran Junction on 18 May 1954. In the left background is the distribution part of the hydro-electric power station at the Assaroe or Cathleen's Falls on the River Erne. The three sidings to the left of the locomotive were used to bring in stone, cement and other supplies for building the large dam and generating house in 1946. The contractors had their own 2'6" gauge railway but, so far as we know, all the transporting from the siding was by road lorry. In the short siding to the right are two cattle wagons at the loading pens.

Below: A general view of Ballyshannon looking west from the road overbridge, probably in September 1957. In the bottom left corner is the gate that sealed off the Down platform for customs work. Beyond the station nameboard and the noticeboard is the customs hut and trestle table. Beyond that again are the shelter and signal cabin, seen in the previous picture. On the Up platform are the main station buildings with the goods store beyond the gents.

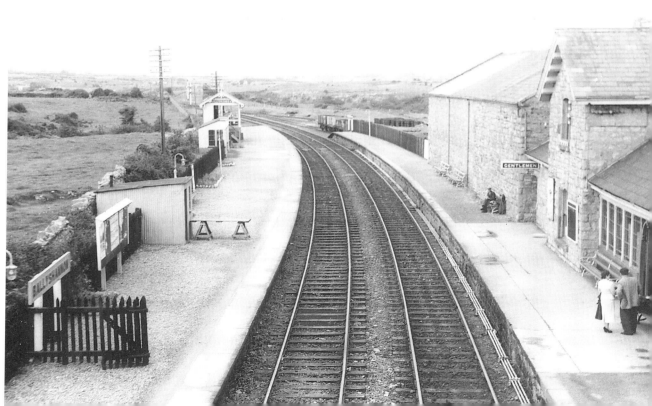

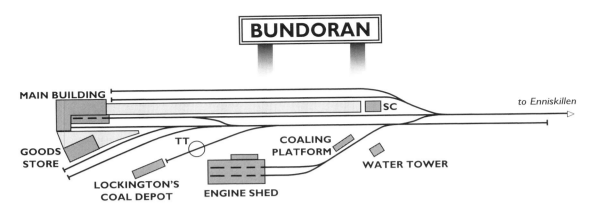

BUNDORAN

MAIN BUILDING

to Enniskillen

SC

GOODS
STORE

TT

COALING
PLATFORM

WATER TOWER

LOCKINGTON'S
COAL DEPOT

ENGINE SHED

Above: Bundoran's passenger building was the only one on the branch in the yellow brick style of WH Mills, the GNR's Civil Engineer. In this unattributed postcard, posted from Bundoran on 4 July 1921, four sidecars and their drivers seem to be waiting for customers off an arriving train. To the right of the main door is the two horse, four-wheel horse bus for the Great Northern Hotel. This ran until the summer of 1929. The building to the right is Bundoran's rarely-photographed goods store.

Opposite bottom: An early 20th century scene showing J class 4-4-0 No 18, after arriving at Bundoran with a passenger train, though the headlamps suggest an empty coaching stock train. Unfortunately no details have survived. This locomotive was named *Hollyhock* before 1914. It was built in 1885, one of a class of twelve and the first of a long line of GNR 4-4-0 locomotives. At one time they were common in Fermanagh and were mostly withdrawn in 1924-9. The exceptions were Nos 118 and 119, which were sold to the Sligo Leitrim in 1921. There they were named *Blacklion* and *Glencar* respectively. *Glencar* was broken up in August 1928 but its boiler survived in *Blacklion* until its withdrawal in 1931. It wasn't actually broken up until June 1937.

Above: Inside Bundoran's one platform train shed in its last summer.

Opposite top: We have to thank the intrepid Ken Nunn, from the south of England, for this rare nineteenth century view of Bundoran. Here we see H class 2-4-0 No 84 with a train of six six wheelers. The guard's raised look-out on the rear vehicle is just visible. The date was 11 September 1898 when the locomotive was just 17 years old. Note the burnished buffers and smokebox straps. The locomotive was later rebuilt and lasted until 1932. It may be that 84 had arrived under the station roof but then set back to clear the engine release crossover. Cattle wagon No 3452, in the sidings on the right, is open all round above shoulder height but, unlike many of its predecessors, it has a roof. Note the fence dividing Bundoran's long finger platform, with the cabin at the far end.

Opposite bottom: P6'6" class 4-4-0 No 73 seems to be about to run round its train after arriving in Bundoran on 14 September 1957 with the 10.45 am Down. The leading coach is a tricomposite brake, followed by an ex-LNWR corridor third, one of a batch purchased from the LMS in 1947. Two passenger vans complete the train. The two tracks in the bottom right corner are sidings whilst the turnout along the right edge leads to the 44-foot diameter turntable. The three bracket signal controlling the approaches to Bundoran is just visible in the extreme right background.

Above: This could have been 10.30 am on any summer's morning but this wet morning is in late September 1957 and scenes such as this were not to be repeated many more times. On the right, U class 4-4-0 No 199 *Lough Derg* has just arrived with the 9.10 am from the Junction (scheduled 10.29 am) and has run up to the buffers of No 2 platform. Note the K^{22} clerestory third, originally 2nd/3rd. On the left PP class 4-4-0 No 50 blows off, impatient to be away with the 10.30 am to Enniskillen, which has a cattle wagon coupled behind the engine. The two men in the right centre of the picture are Benny Nolan and a plumber called Lynn from Enniskillen. Driver Paddy Gallagher is just discernable in 199's cab.

Below: Bundoran looks busy in this Sunday evening view, taken on 8 July 1956, showing PP class 4-4-0 No 106 ready to leave with a 'Hills of Donegal' excursion returning to Belfast. The seven or eight coach train includes a modern flush panelled buffet car. In the left background, visible in the siding alongside the train shed, is a four coach train with roof boards, probably the stock of the 'Bundoran Express'. At platform 2, and the siding behind are at least three separate trains — probably excursions waiting to leave later that evening. The coach on the right is is a class J[6] brake composite, with centre corridor accommodation in the third class end and side corridor for first. Just visible, in the right background, is a large corrugated iron and wood pavilion towering above the bus depot. The pavilion was used by some excursions for picnic lunches.

Opposite top: This delightful scene has been published before but fully deserves another airing. The date is 3 June 1954 and shows railcar C³ and No 204 *Antrim* outside Bundoran shed, with AL class 0-6-0 No 59 visible beyond the shed. The railcar has worked in on the 9.10 am from the Junction and will return on the 2.25 pm to Enniskillen, calling, as required, at several crossings. These were Crowe's, Castle Archdale and Johnston's, between Kesh and Irvinestown and Tague's, in the Irvinestown to Bundoran Junction section. In addition, the railcar will stop at Legg's Crossing, between Pettigo and Castlecaldwell, for mails only. As indicated by the nameboard, 204 will work the Up 'Bundoran Express' (due away at 12.20 pm) The 0-6-0 had arrived with the 5.50 am goods from Enniskillen, due here at 10.20 am. After shunting, 59 has been turned and is sitting in the siding off the turntable, probably to have its fire cleaned before leaving at 11.50 am on the goods for Enniskillen, where it wasn't due until 6.12 pm. A couple of passenger vans are just visible at the loading bank, alongside the passenger train shed.

Above: A classic posed shot of driver Paddy Martin (right) and his fireman on the running board of PP class 4-4-0 No 46 on 22 April 1953. The locomotive is sitting on the loop and has probably just taken water from the column on the extreme left. The lazy black smoke suggests that the locomotive is brewing up before working the 10.30 am to Enniskillen. Bundoran cabin is visible behind the tender.

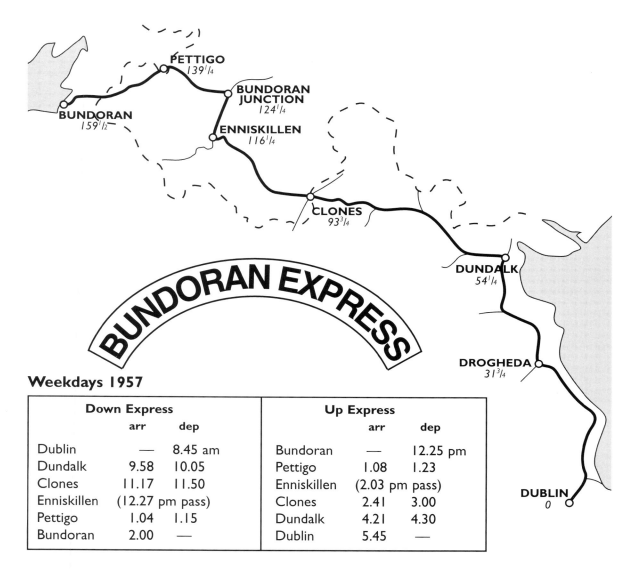

PETTIGO
139¹/₄

BUNDORAN
JUNCTION
124¹/₄

BUNDORAN
159¹/₂

ENNISKILLEN
116¹/₄

CLONES
93³/₄

DUNDALK
54¹/₄

DROGHEDA
31³/₄

DUBLIN
0

BUNDORAN EXPRESS

Weekdays 1957

Down Express			Up Express		
	arr	dep		arr	dep
Dublin	—	8.45 am	Bundoran	—	12.25 pm
Dundalk	9.58	10.05	Pettigo	1.08	1.23
Clones	11.17	11.50	Enniskillen	(2.03 pm pass)	
Enniskillen	(12.27 pm pass)		Clones	2.41	3.00
Pettigo	1.04	1.15	Dundalk	4.21	4.30
Bundoran	2.00	—	Dublin	5.45	—

Opposite top: VS class 3-cyl 4-4-0 No 206 *Liffey* passing Harmonstown, on the outskirts of Dublin, with the Down 'Bundoran Express', probably in 1956. Unusually the train is only three coaches long and does not include any refreshment vehicle. The train may be a relief (a second portion following the main train).

Opposite bottom: The Down 'Bundoran Express' waiting at Clones on 10 June 1950, around 11.15 am. Emphasising the variety of motive power on this train, the locomotive is UG class 0-6-0 No 148, built in 1948, and the load is the more usual seven bogies. The leading vehicle is an M[1] full brake, followed by several modern flush panelled coaches — four K[15] thirds and an F[16] composite. At the tail of the train is the brake composite from Belfast, added here in place of the buffet car, which had come on the train from Dublin and was now detached to await the Up 'Express', due at 3 pm. This layover of the buffet car would be frowned upon by today's accountants. However, to change the buffet car over at Pettigo would have been operationally difficult, with three trains in the station.

Opposite top: This has for long been one of my favourite photographs; it brings back so much and I feel I could just walk into the scene. It is Monday 31 May 1954 and No 204 drifts in with the Down 'Express'. The driver is Paddy McKeown and the fireman, holding the staff, is Denis Cosgrove. Neil Sprinks was fortunate to get this superb shot, as the Lough Derg season had commenced the previous Saturday that year, instead of the normal 1 June. Being so early in the season, the train is another lightweight — an M^1 van, an F^{16} compo, a K^{15} third and a brake compo. As the 'Express' was not supposed to stop in Northern Ireland precautions were needed to avoid a signal check. Sometimes the Lisnaskea signalman tied a luggage label to the staff saying, "Take your time — Enniskillen not ready." The label, of course, went in the firebox! On a personal note, the Tempo Road is visible behind the telegraph poles and the sharp-eyed may just make out the Killynure siding just right of the signal pole, with a string of cattle wagons in it.

Opposite bottom: On a Sunday in August 1957, U class 4-4-0 No 201 *Meath* has arrived at Bundoran with the 'Express' and has set back to clear the engine release crossover — the driver seems to be winding the engine into forward gear again so that it can move forward to run round. Soon *Meath* will have shunted the train to the siding behind platform 2 and will then go to the shed to be turned, serviced and 'put to bed' until its next turn of duty, which will be the following day's Up 'Express', which she will work to Dundalk. The view to the left is dominated by Bundoran UDC's water tank.

Above: Pettigo, with Up and Down 'Expresses' crossing on 1 September 1956. The Dublin-bound Up 'Express' is in the charge of No 202 *Louth*. The locomotive is probably taking water before starting its 45½ non-stop run through Fermanagh (and a bit of Tyrone). The border was at the next bridge under the line, about 200 yards ahead of the train. The steam blowing below the bufferbeam is from the cylinder drain cocks and suggests that either the train has just come to a stop or there is a leak in the regulator valve.

Opposite top: Having re-entered the Irish Republic near Clones, and taken water, the 'Bundoran Express' is seen here pulling out of Clones to head for Dundalk, hauled by No 198 *Lough Swilly*. The coach to the right is an ex Dundalk, Newry and Greenore Railway 6-wheel brake — a classic LNWR designed vehicle. This line, originally owned by the LNWR, used the old pre-1923 London North Western livery right up to the 1950s.

Opposite bottom: Whilst the small U class 4-4-0s, with their 5'9" driving wheels, were usual 'Express' motive power west of Dundalk (because of weight restrictions), south of Dundalk could see literally anything. Here one of the superb S class engines — No 170 *Errigal* — is being prepared at Dundalk running shed to work the Dundalk to Dublin section. To the right is one of the high-sided coal wagons of 15 tons capacity and clearly labelled 'LOCO'.

Above: Journey — and pilgrimage too, perhaps — almost over. An Up 'Bundoran Express' rolls into Dublin (Amiens Street) behind QL class 4-4-0 No 128 at an unknown date in the 1950s. On this side of the engine the fireman has time for a cigarette, the hard work now behind him. The K^{12} buffet car is immediately behind the locomotive and one of its attendants, his work also done, is leaning from a window.

THE SLIGO LEITRIM AND NORTHERN COUNTIES RAILWAY

Below: It is now time to retrace our steps to Fermanagh's county town and examine the Sligo Leitrim and Northern Counties. We begin near the Great Northern's Enniskillen South signal cabin, seen here on the left. Below it, the GNR line from Clones is in the cutting, with an oil lamp marking the spot where the single line staff for the section to or from Lisbellaw was handed over. The building in the centre of the picture is the Sligo Leitrim's Head Office including the General Manager's office. It was made of unpretentious corrugated iron and usually painted a brownish red colour. It appears in some SLNCR documents as 'Chief Office'. There is some evidence to suggest that the platform on which the Head Office sits was the Sligo Leitrim's original passenger station, but the best verdict seems to be 'case not proven'. The track past this platform was the only connection between the GNR and SLNCR tracks — note the change from chaired track to flat-bottom rail. In the centre foreground is a remarkable movable diamond crossing, a rare item of trackwork. This picture dates from about 1932.

Above: This is a view from the South cabin on 6 August 1937. The track in the bottom left corner of the picture leads to the SLNCR turntable. In the sidings in the distance, seven-ton open wagons 139 and 76 flank a train of three six-wheel carriages. The six-wheel brake coach in the foreground is an ex GNR vehicle. Above it the SLNCR main line can be seen curving past the two Sligo Leitrim engine sheds, one of which contains *Lough Gill*. The bridge over the Tempo Road was immediately past the further shed. The white painted signal, seen here, was beyond the bridge. Another signal in the right background marks where the SLNCR curved away to the south en route for Castlecoole and Sligo. The nearer engine shed — known as the 'large shed' — was another corrugated iron structure.The coal unloading bank, mentioned in 'Charles Remembers' was the siding running behind the large shed.

Opposite top: This view is almost back to back with the previous picture. Here *Enniskillen* — built in 1905 and the second of three 'Sir Henry' class engines — is shunting in the Sligo Leitrim yard on 27 September 1957. Immediately behind the locomotive is 7-ton brake van No 6, followed by brake composite coach No 9, two cattle wagons and two loaded open wagons. Part of the County Hospital (see 'Charles Remembers') is visible above Enniskillen's chimney.

Opposite bottom: *Lough Erne* is seen here getting away from Enniskillen with the 7.20 pm mixed to Sligo on 31 May 1954. Bogie brake compo No 9 was a regular feature on this train and is followed by four cattle wagons (one of them unroofed), two open wagons and a brake van. On the extreme right is the SLNCR turntable, with what looks like a diesel fuel pump on the embankment.

Above: In September 1957, looking from the Sligo Leitrim yard towards the station, we see *Sir Henry* between duties and waiting at the Head Office platform. In the background a Great Northern train has arrived from Clones, whilst SLNCR railbus 2A waits to leave, probably on the 12 noon to Sligo. The movable diamond crossing can be seen to the left of the engine.

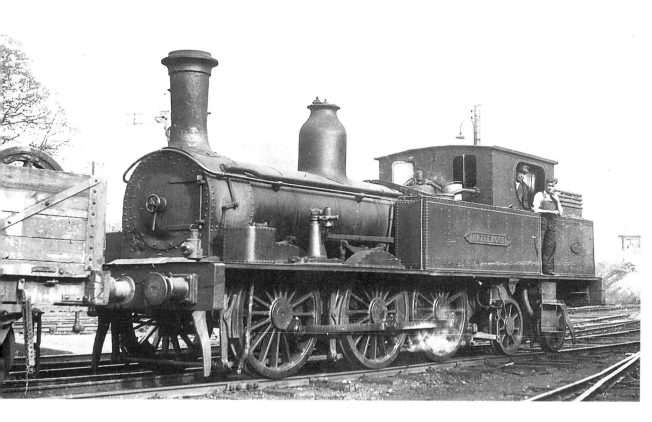

Opposite top: Hazlewood was built in 1899. It was the last of the five 'Leitrim' class 0-6-4T locomotives to be built and the only one to survive until 1957. Apart from the addition of coal rails, the only visible change since its construction was a different cab shape, resulting from a malicious derailment in 1923, during the Irish Civil War. The cylinder visible below the water tank, above the leading bogie wheel, was one of two that operated the locomotive's steam brake. The wheel arrangement was an unusual choice in Ireland for main line use; almost all other classes of 0-6-4T were built for shunting in goods yards or dock lines. The Sligo Leitrim had ten locomotives with this wheel arrangement and seemed to have little reason to try anything else. If anything, the two ex-Great Northern 4-4-0s used on the line in the 1920s were not suited to the job in hand.

Opposite bottom: Lissadell waits to leave Enniskillen with six-wheel coach No 3 on 17 May 1950. Unfortunately no other details of this interesting working have survived. At the GNR platform, to the right, are a cattle wagon and horsebox. *Lissadell*, also built in 1899, was a sister of *Hazlewood*, seen in the previous picture.

Above: A side view of *Sir Henry* in 1948 on the turntable at Enniskillen. Incidentally this was the only turntable owned by the SLNCR, since Manorhamilton did not have one and the GSR/CIE table was used at Sligo. The building to the left is the SLNCR's Head Office. Enniskillen South cabin was unusual in being glazed on all four sides rather than the more usual three. This was because it controlled Sligo trains as well as GNR ones and an all-round view was essential. *Sir Henry* was built in 1904 and reboilered in 1929.

Opposite top: The SLNCR used railbuses for many of its passenger services. The first was Railbus A, delivered to the Sligo Leitrim on 20 June 1935 and converted from an older GNR Associated Daimler Type 413 road bus, with an AEC petrol engine. Like many buses from this manufacturer, the vehicle had a full width cab. It was fitted with Howden-Meredith patent wheels. This type of wheel, devised at Dundalk, allowed the bus to retain its pneumatic road tyres but now inside a railway profiled tyre. This allowed the bus to retain all the characteristics of road suspension. Above each wheel rim was a detector that would activate the brakes if the pneumatic tyre deflated. In 1938 it was fitted with a Gardner 4LW diesel engine.

Opposite bottom: The original Railbus A had only been converted to diesel propulsion for about a year when, on 7 March 1939, it was runner-up in a tussle with a steam locomotive. Its replacement was an even older railbus (Ex-GNR D1), dating from 1926. The diesel engine of the original 'A' was reused.

Above: By December 1950 a replacement body for Railbus A was required and another GNR bus body was pressed into service on the same chassis. With this body, the revitalised 'A' is seen on Enniskillen's turntable, along with its luggage trailer. The trailer was built at Manorhamilton in 1942 using the bogie off a scrapped Great Southern Railway Sentinel steam railcar.

Opposite top: This is Railbus 2A, another Dundalk conversion of a GNR road bus, but this time with a Gardner diesel engine from the start. It arrived on the line in early 1938 with a new body and, although similar to the last metamorphosis of 'A', had many detail differences. In these pictures you can see '2A''s outward sweep at the bottom of the side panels, compared to 'A''s inward sweep, as well as many differences around the fronts of the vehicles. In the dock platform, on the left, is one of the 1924 bogie coaches. Most likely it is No 10, the coach that worked on the 10.20 am Sligo to Enniskillen and the 1.40 pm return. As it always, therefore, ran during daylight hours, it wasn't equipped with any form of lighting! Latterly a coach stabled here would have been for the 7.20 pm mixed to Sligo (see page 129).

Opposite bottom: The pride of the line was Railcar B. Built by Walkers of Wigan, 'B' was an articulated vehicle after the style of the GNR 'C' cars or the pioneer Clogher Valley Railcar 1 seen earlier (page 26). This is the powered end, with a spacious driver's cab and engine, carried on a 4-wheel bogie. The passenger section included a sizable area for luggage and parcels accessed by the double doors. The door at the further end included retractable steps for use at level crossings. The radiator for the diesel engine was carried on the roof at this end. For a view of the opposite end of Railcar B see page 132.

Above: *Lough Erne* has just arrived in Enniskillen with the 6.30 am goods from Sligo (due here at 10.00 am) on 31 May 1954 and is starting to shunt the train back into the sidings that have access to the GNR. The GNR engine shed is on the extreme left and the roof of Enniskillen South cabin is just visible above the first wagon. *Lough Erne* was built in 1949 and was one of the last two engines built for the SLNCR, its sister being *Lough Melvin*.

Opposite top: The Sligo Leitrim had two engine sheds at Enniskillen, as we have already seen. This brick-built shed housed the steam engine based here. On 24 June 1937 the locomotive in residence was *Sligo*, the first of two engines to carry the name. This locomotive had been GNR A class 0-6-0 No 49 until 1931, when the Sligo Leitrim bought it. It was replaced in 1941 by sister locomotive No 69 which was also named *Sligo*. Note the brickwork on the corner of the shed, stepped to clear the loading gauge of the nearby running lines. The very small metal bridge over the Tempo Road (SLNCR bridge No 1) is visible behind and to the left of the shed. The longer corrugated iron shed, on the right, was later the overnight stabling point for Railcar B.

Opposite bottom: On 21 July 1954, 0-6-4T *Lough Melvin* shunts a train of six-wheelers at the SLNCR yard. The carriages appear to be Nos 2, 3 and 4, in order from the locomotive. This was the stock of the 4 pm from Sligo, a steam working having been substituted for Railcar B, which had failed at Florencecourt (see page 132). The gent in the foreground is Mr E W Monaghan, the SLNCR General Manager. The GNR line from Clones is on the left and, once again, the Head Office building. The SLNCR goods store is on the right.

Above: It is 2 June 1954, about 10.00 am, and *Lough Melvin* threads her way along the edge of the Castlecoole Woods, near the Castlecoole Road bridge, with the 6.30 am goods from Sligo. The train is mostly cattle wagons, of course.

Opposite top: The unmistakable Weirs Bridge at Killyhevlin, officially bridge No 4 (No 2 was under the Castlecoole Road and No 3 over the Dublin Road). The bridge took its name from Scarlett's eel weirs, which were here until a drainage scheme was carried out in 1846. This is the better known view from the Dublin Road looking south. The bridge was built by Courtney, Stephens and Bailey from Dublin. In its 467 feet length was a mixture of masonry abutments and cast iron pillars with lattice girder spans between. Despite its fine appearance, the bridge had a speed limit of just 5 mph and engines had to shut off steam while crossing it. This view was taken about 1932.

Opposite bottom: This view is from the opposite, or southern, end of the bridge and shows *Sir Henry* setting out for Sligo with the 2 pm goods on 20 July 1956. The wagon next the engine is a horse box, while the first, lighter coloured, van in the middle of the bridge is a Great Northern cement van, based in Drogheda. Between the piers can be seen a bucket dredger and other plant used in deepening the river to help alleviate flooding.

Above: Yet another delightful scene from the camera of Neil Sprinks. We are at the south end of the Weirs Bridge as *Lough Erne*, with a lightly loaded 7.20 pm mixed train for Sligo crosses on 31 May 1954. The train was known as a 'mixed' because it conveyed both passengers and goods. Here the passenger accommodation (as always) is provided by bogie brake composite No 9. There must not have been any goods wagons needing to be moved from Enniskillen that evening, so the train is completed by only a goods brake van. Note the bridge number painted on the masonry pier to the left.

Above: This is near level crossing No 2 — or 'No 2 gates' to the railwaymen — where the line crossed the minor road to Drumkeen and Stinson's Bridge. The train is the 6.30 am goods from Sligo, made up of covered vans from CIE, the GNR and some from the SLNCR. The locomotive is *Sir Henry* and the date was 26 June 1957. High on a hill above the back of the train is the signal guarding No 3 gates at Mullaghy on the Enniskillen to Swanlinbar road.

Below: *Lough Erne* is seen here stopped near Florencecourt while working a goods from Enniskillen to Sligo on 18 April 1955. The second wagon contains stone ballast and this is being shovelled over the side for later use on the track. While this saved the expense of working a separate ballast train (as on most other railways), it had an adverse effect on timekeeping.

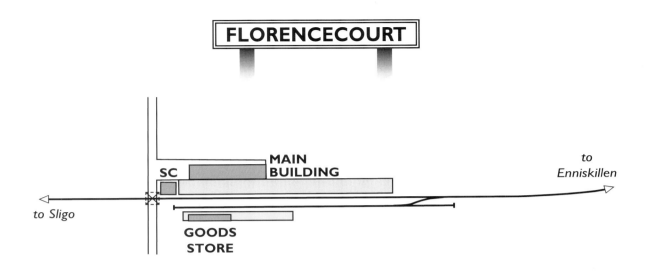

FLORENCECOURT

SC

MAIN
BUILDING

to Sligo

GOODS
STORE

to Enniskillen

Below: This is Florencecourt looking towards Belcoo in 1956. There was one passenger platform, with the signal cabin at the far end controlling a level crossing. Access to the siding on the left, with its goods store, was from the Enniskillen end of the station.

Above: An interesting view, taken on 21 July 1954, showing Railcar B, which was working the 12 noon to Sligo. The brakes of the railcar had seized at a level crossing just beyond Florencecourt and *Lough Melvin,* sent from Enniskillen, has hauled it back to Florencecourt. The passengers have been obliged to disgorge both their luggage and themselves so that the railcar can be shunted to a siding.

Below: Lough Melvin is now shunting the railcar into the siding. The passengers proceeded to Sligo on the 2 pm railbus, which was presumably rather full! The railcar had hidden couplings behind the front and rear panelling to enable it to be hauled.

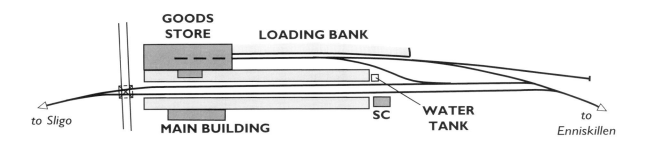

GOODS
STORE   LOADING BANK

to Sligo   MAIN BUILDING   SC   WATER
TANK   to
Enniskillen

Above: Belcoo, in 1956, looking towards Enniskillen. Railcar B is probably on the 9.30 am ex Sligo. In this view we can see the main station building with its awning on the Down platform. On the extreme left is the goods store and the waiting room on the Up platform.

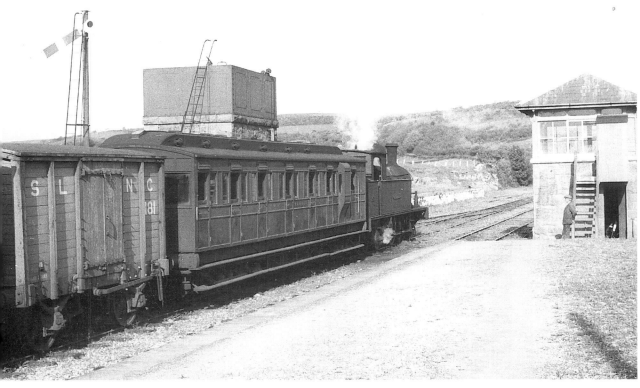

Opposite top: This second view, looking in the same direction, but from the opposite side of the line, allows us to look along the Down platform towards the signal cabin. On the Up side the water tower is now visible and the goods yard is occupied by some cattle trucks and an open wagon. Railcar B is about to depart, probably on the 9.30 am ex Sligo, which reached Belcoo about 11.05 am and is due in Enniskillen at 11.40am.

Opposite bottom: The Enniskillen end of Belcoo on 26 September 1957. *Enniskillen,* with the 9 am goods from Sligo, is taking water from the tank on the left. The coach is again bogie compo No 9 and is being worked empty to Enniskillen for use on the 7.20 pm mixed. Beyond the locomotive is part of the goods yard, which handled considerable Free to Free goods traffic. This was an arrangement arrived at in 1936, whereby goods from the Irish Free State could be shipped through Northern Ireland in sealed wagons for delivery to customers in another part of the Irish Free State — hence the name. Belcoo was, of course, the railhead for Blacklion in County Leitrim. Belcoo's signal cabin, main station building and Down platform have recently been restored by their proud owner, Miss Mairead O'Dolan.

Above: The 7.20 pm Sligo-bound mixed train pauses at Belcoo on 21 July 1954. The locomotive is *Lough Melvin* and the train is composed of two six-wheelers, bogie coach No 9, a couple of cattle wagons and a brake van. The six-wheelers were being returned to Sligo after use on the 4 pm Up train, when the failure of Railcar B resulted in a steam substitution (see pages 126 and 132). Some goods wagons are visible in the goods yard in the left background, and the home signal is still in the off position.

Fermanagh Bus Services

SLNCR Buses

Our bus section covers the operations of four bus companies which operated in or into Fermanagh. We begin with the SLNCR and specifically with the last two buses operated by Hezekiah Appleby, who was related to my co-author Norman.

Opposite top: On 13 August 1948 we see an ex Appleby bus at Manorhamilton, Co Leitrim. The last two Appleby buses were bought by the SLNCR on 2 April 1945. EI 3905 was a 1938 Bedford with 29 seats and has been lettered 'SL&NCR', though it is still actually in Appleby livery.

Below: The other Appleby bus was IL 2058, a Bedford WLB built in 1932 and seating twenty, also seen at Manorhamilton on the same date. It has been repainted into SLNCR livery. Towards the end of 1948, both Appleby buses were replaced by new Commers.

Below: This is Manorhamilton garage, where the SLNCR buses were serviced and maintained. On 8 June 1953, EI 5040 is inside the garage. This bus was a 32 seater Commer Commando with a diesel engine, built in 1948, to replace one of the Appleby buses.

Above: The other new Commer of 1948 was EI 4907, also a 32 seater Commando, and seen on the same date at Manorhamilton. The SLNCR livery was of dark and light green.

Erne Bus Service

Opposite top: Two Erne buses are visible in this 18 August 1948 view at the Diamond, near Enniskillen's Town Hall. Nearer the camera is ZI 8748, a 1932-3 built Leyland Lion LT4, purchased second hand from CIE. On the opposite side of High Street is sister Leyland ZI 8744. The rear of this vehicle shows the attractive Erne Bus Service scrolling, the livery of this fleet being cream and brown.

Opposite bottom: Bundoran, on 14 August 1948, with the Atlantic as a backdrop. ZI 8744, still with its original GSR rear entrance body, is waiting for its return trip to Enniskillen. The steeply raked driver's windscreen and low roof profile were very typical of early 1930s bus design. Note the starting handle, which was designed to rest in a 'handle down' position when not in use and remained like this even while the vehicle was in motion.

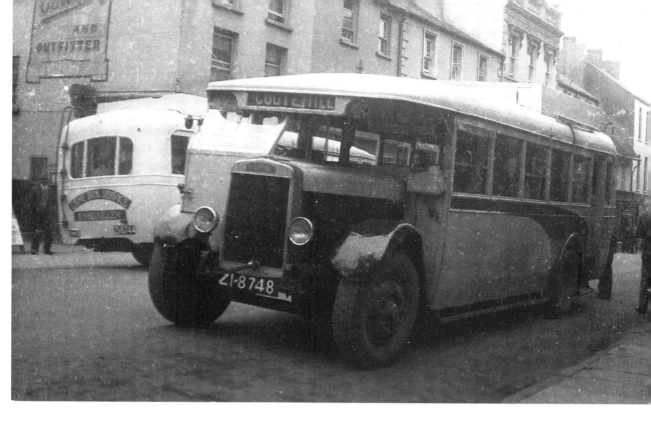

Opposite top: This more modern looking vehicle is in fact another early 1930s Leyland Lion which has been fitted with a new front entrance body. It was originally built for the Great Southern Railways and is seen here at Bundoran on 14 August 1948.

Opposite bottom: IL 5698, a 1952 front entrance Leyland Royal Tiger PSU with Saunders-Roe body, was the most modern bus in the Erne fleet. In this 1957 view we see it at Custom House Quay, Dublin, when it was on private hire duty, along with IL 5414, a 1951 front entrance Leyland Comet. Behind the Erne buses is a UTA Leyland Tiger Cub coach.

Above: The Erne Bus Service's garage at Enniskillen was in Quay Lane, opposite the gasworks. Here, in this 8 June 1953 view, we see a rear aspect of IL 5698. By this date, the two oldest Tigers — ZI 8744 and ZI 8748 — were lying derelict outside the garage.

GNR Buses

Above: GNR No 242 (ZC 4102), another single deck Gardner, parked at Enniskillen station on 18 May 1950. No 242 was built in 1938 and had a GNR body. The building in the background is Creighton's furniture shop (now demolished).

Below: GNR single deck Gardner-engined bus No 368 (IY 6182) in Railway Street, Enniskillen, parked outside the station. This bus was built in 1949 with a Harkness body. Note the layout of the windows in comparison to No 242.

NIRTB Buses

Above: Pettigo was divided by a river, out of sight to the left, which also marked the political border between the Irish Free State and Northern Ireland after 1921. That part of the town that was in Northern Ireland was called Tullyhommon. Here three Leyland PS1s, on private hire, are waiting close to the border on 2 August 1950. They may be waiting to pick up a party of pilgrims visiting Lough Derg, near Pettigo. At the front is MZ 1809, built in 1948, one of the last to be completed in NIRTB colours.

Below: At the old UTA bus depot at Eden Street, Enniskillen, the main subject of this photo is L 300, a Commer Beadle demonstrator, a one off, built in 1957, and just arrived in from Belfast. Also visible is Z 772 a 1946 Leyland PS1, about to set out for Fivemiletown. The bus behind L 300 is probably another PS1.

Photo Credits

Bibliography

John Aldridge   *British Buses Before 1945*, Shepperton, 1955.
R M Arnold   *The Golden Years of the Great Northern Railway, Part One*, Belfast, 1976.
G I Millar   *Fifty Years of Public Service*, Belfast, 1985.
E M Patterson   *The Clogher Valley Railway*, Newton Abbot, 1972.
E M Patterson   *The Great Northern Railway of Ireland*, Newton Abbot, 1962.
N W Sprinks   *The Sligo, Leitrim and Northern Counties Railway*, Billericay, 1970.

Rear cover photographs:

Main: Q Class 4-4-0 No 122 at Enniskillen shed in June 1957.

Inset: SLNCR 0-6-4T *Sir Henry* at Belcoo in May 1957.